Australian Aboriginal Art

Australian Aboriginal Art

The art of the Alligator Rivers region, Northern Territory

Robert Edwards

Australian Institute of Aboriginal Studies

Canberra 1979

Published in Australia by the
Australian Institute of Aboriginal Studies
P.O. Box 553, Canberra City, A.C.T. 2601

Sold and distributed in North and South America by
Humanities Press Inc.
171 First Avenue, Atlantic Highlands, N.J. 07716

PUBLISHER'S NOTE: The text of this book, except for the introduction
and the omission of appendices, is identical to that published by the
same author in 1974 under the title, *The Art of the Alligator Rivers
Region,* as part of the Alligator Rivers Region Environmental Fact
Finding Study. This edition features more colour plates than the
original, a revised introduction and has minor revisions to some picture
captions.

AIAS new series no. 15

National Library of Australia card number and ISBN 0 85575 105 3 (soft cover)
0 85575 106 1 (hard cover)
USA edition ISBN 0 391 01611 3 (soft cover)
0 391 01610 5 (hard cover)

Printed in Australia by The Dominion Press, Melbourne.

7.79.5000

COVER DESIGN by Stephen Cole from colour transparencies supplied
by Darrell Lewis. *Front:* X-ray kangaroos at Stag Creek Gallery.
Back: X-ray female figure also at the Stag Creek Gallery.

Contents

Illustrations

Introduction

The remote Alligator Rivers Region described in this volume is situated east of Darwin on the western edge of Arnhem Land. It comprises the entire watershed of the East Alligator River and Cooper Creek, and also the catchments east of the South Alligator River. The total area is 19 000 km² of which a large section in the east is within the Arnhem Land Aboriginal Reserve. A smaller reserve, known as Woolwonga, is also involved. The Aboriginal population of approximately 700 is centred at Oenpelli, with many families scattered throughout the bush in small outstations.

For many years there has been a growing awareness of the Region's highly diverse wildlife and native flora and its vast galleries of Aboriginal rock paintings. Attention recently has focused on the large reserves of uranium discovered in the area and there is an increasing concern for the preservation of Aboriginal art sites of particular significance as well as natural areas of religious importance to Aboriginal groups. The establishment of a National Park in the Alligator Rivers Region was first proposed in 1965 by the Northern Territory Reserves Board. However, many conflicting interests needed to be resolved; the area encompassed an Aboriginal Reserve and a wildlife sanctuary as well as existing special purpose leases and pastoral and mining activities. Although a National Park was approved in principle in 1969, two pastoral leases and a number of prospecting authorities were issued after that time, indicating that the government remained ambivalent in its intentions. However, in 1970 the government appointed a planning team to prepare detailed plans for a major National Park in Arnhem Land.

The team was to formulate a broad framework for a long term development, recommend the most suitable boundaries for the proposed park, list in detail the aspects of interest, make suggestions for overall future development and conservation and comment on needs and a timetable for road, air and water access. The team studied a base area of 2 590 km² in the

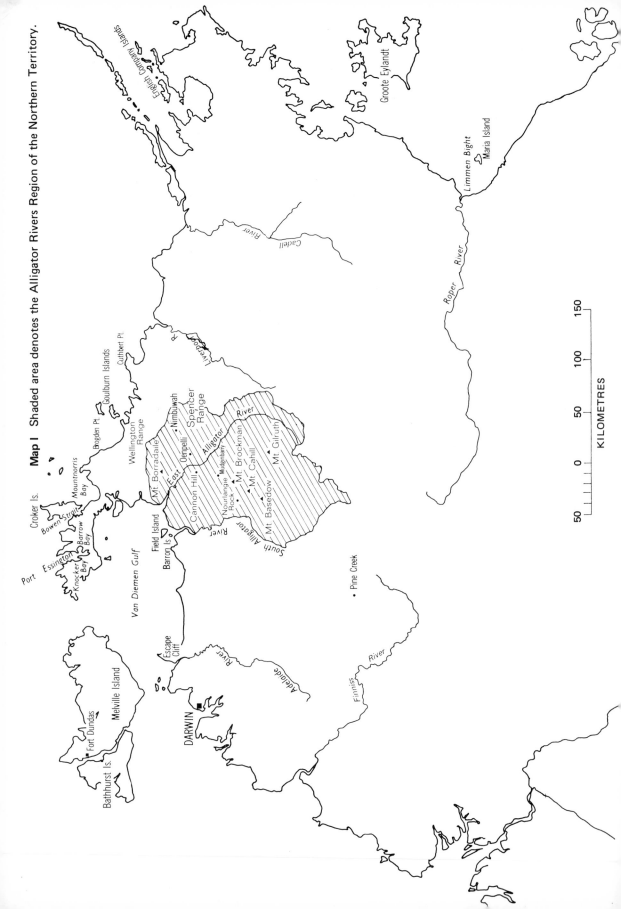

Map I Shaded area denotes the Alligator Rivers Region of the Northern Territory.

catchment of the East and South Alligator Rivers. Their report was published in February 1972. However, at this time huge uranium deposits were found in the Mt Brockman area, followed by further discoveries at Nabarlek, Nourlangie and south of Cannon Hill. This indicated that much more factual information was needed in order to ensure that any decisions for development in the Region were based on a sound knowledge of the environmental consequences of such decisions.

In April 1972 the government and the mining industry formed a joint committee to undertake the Alligator Rivers Region Environmental Fact Finding Study. The Study involved the participation of the Departments of the Northern Territory, Health, and Northern Development, the (then) Bureau of Mineral Resources, CSIRO, Atomic Energy Commission, individual mining companies with interests in the area, the Australian Conservation Foundation and consultants. Twelve separate studies were undertaken with a view to providing basic scientific facts about the Region; they were not studies of the impact of developments which might occur. The Study was managed by an Executive Committee and advised by a Scientific and Technical Evaluation Committee. A Review Report was presented by the Executive Committee on the completion of the Study.

This volume on the rock art of the Alligator Rivers Region is one of the reports which made up the comprehensive study of this remote region of Australia. Since the publication of the first edition in 1974, the Alligator Rivers Area, and more specifically the Kakadu National Park, has been brought almost daily to the attention of the Australian public as the moves to commence uranium mining in the area intensified. The emergence of large mining townships is now inevitable as the Ranger Project commences its operations, and other mining companies complete negotiations to follow suit.

The Kakadu National Park became a reality with its proclamation by the Federal Government. But this alone will not ensure protection for the rich art heritage of the area or of the aspirations of the local Aboriginal population to maintain their own cultural identity. The park lies next to the richest uranium deposits yet discovered in the world, and the development of these will have far-reaching effects on the area and on its Aboriginal inhabitants.

Roads linking these townships to the capital of Darwin will be much busier than the road which now leads to the mining exploration sites. Inaccessibility has minimised vandalism of the cave paintings so far but as numbers of visitors increase the inevitable writing or carving of names and other forms of damage are certain to become serious unless adequate protection measures are adopted.

Bus tours to selected easily accessible cave art sites are operated from Darwin already and tourism organisations are mobilised to take advantage

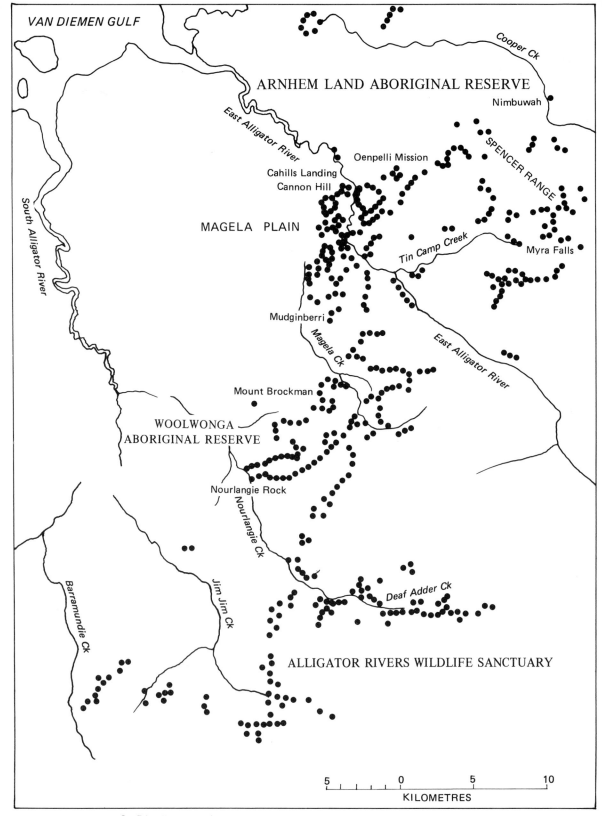

Map 2 Distribution of cave painting sites located in the Alligator Rivers Region.

of the obvious potential of the Kakadu area as a major tourist drawcard. The planned townships to be built in close proximity to the Kakadu National Park and the projected increase in population of the area will place immediate pressure on the resources of the Park and its Rangers. As roads pass close to major sites tourists, picnickers or travellers may unwittingly enter sacred areas or desecrate important sacred sites.

The Kakadu National Park is a magnificent area of natural wilderness containing varieties of wildlife and plant species not found elsewhere. It encompasses hundreds of galleries of Aboriginal rock paintings varying in antiquity from tens of thousands of years to the present decade. These galleries are among the finest in the world and provide continuous evidence of the occupation of the Australian continent by man from the Pleistocene epoch to the present. It should be the duty not only of Australia but also of the international community through UNESCO to preserve and maintain the Park and its art as a world cultural heritage before the proximity of townships, rapid tourist development as well as unchecked natural deterioration of rock painting galleries take their toll and severely deplenish this great heritage of the art of mankind.

The national programme of site recording was to run initially for five years. At its Biennial Conference in May 1978, the Council of the Australian Institute of Aboriginal Studies decided to continue to assist the various State and Territory authorities in the recording of Aboriginal sites. Grants continue to be made through the Sites of Significance Advisory Committee mentioned on Page 178. The structure of the committee has changed since the initial publication of this book. It is now elected by the Council of the Australian Institute of Aboriginal Studies each two years, not on a State representation basis, but on the basis of expertise required for the diverse aspects of the programme.

Robert Edwards
Sydney,
April, 1979

Acknowledgements

The survey of art sites in the Alligator Rivers Region was facilitated by numerous individuals who gave generously of their time, knowledge and experience.

Particular thanks are due to George Chaloupka who provided valuable information for inclusion in the report. Important data was supplied also by the (late) Eric Brandl, an authority on the art of the Deaf Adder Creek Valley and other sites in Arnhem Land and author of *Australian Aboriginal paintings in western and central Arnhem Land*.

The Oenpelli Council met on several occasions to discuss the survey and to offer guidance. Members of the community assisted in many ways and Alf Wilson (superintendent) and Peter Carroll (linguist) took endless trouble to facilitate the project.

The field survey was aided by the management and staff of mining companies operating in the Alligator Rivers Region, in particular Noranda, Geopeko and Pan Continental. Owen Marshall (Noranda), Don Woods (Geopeko) and Terry Walls (Australian Mining Industry Council) gave special attention to my many requests for help.

Doug Bannear, George Chaloupka and Anthony Wallis shared fieldwork with me in the Alligator Rivers Region and rendered practical assistance, often under difficult circumstances.

Among the many individuals who co-operated closely in the project are: John Calaby (CSIRO), Chris Christian (author of *Review Report*), Neil Conway and Max Giles (Atomic Energy Commission), Terry Hanley (Study Logistics Officer), Colin Jack-Hinton (Northern Territory Museums), John Lake and David Lindner (National Parks), Ray McHenry and Ted Evans (Department of Aboriginal Affairs), Alan O'Brien (Department of the Northern Territory) and Frank Woerle (Cannon Hill Ranger). Lyall Gillespie, the initial co-ordinator of the study and John Laurie, who later accepted the heavy responsibility of this position, facilitated the field study and offered practical advice.

Kristin Munday commented on the manuscript and Rosemary Kennemore checked the bibliography.

Photographs were made available by George Chaloupka: Plates 4, 13, 18 (top), 31, 32, 37 (top), 39, 40 (top); Charles P. Mountford: Plate 15 (bottom); Ederic Slater: Plates 5 and 25; Darrell Lewis, Cover; E. J. Brandl: Plate 30; Department of the Northern Territory: Plate 6 (top); C. S. Christian: Plate 6 (bottom); the Lands Survey Branch of the Department of the Northern Territory: Plates 13 and 18 (bottom); the Ministry of Public Building and Works, London: Plate 44. Other photographs are by the author. The engraving of Port Essington reproduced in Plate 3 is by Dumont D'urville.

Denis Marfleet of Magill, South Australia, prepared colour enlargements; special attention was paid to production of the original report by Delmont Pty Ltd, South Australia.

Professor John Mulvaney, Dr Peter Ucko and Professor Derek Freeman offered constructive criticism and encouragement throughout the project.

CHAPTER 1

Historical Background

Aboriginal art in the Alligator Rivers Region is to a large extent the only record of the history of the area since the arrival of Aborigines in north Australia 25 000 and more years ago.

Sacred figures painted in many rock shelter galleries were believed by Aborigines to be the work of legendary heroes of their Dreamtime. Myths associated with such paintings tell of the formation of the landscape and perpetuate a link between the mythological past and the present.

Shelters richly decorated with paintings record the daily life of the Aborigines of the region, while the numerous figures depicting aspects of contact with the outside world tell a graphic story of the arrival of new cultures in north Australia and their profound affect upon Aboriginal Society.

As an introduction to a complete understanding of this extensive body of art it is necessary first to retrace the story of discovery and exploration in north Australia.

Exploration by Sea

The first substantiated sighting of Australia was in 1606, when Willem Jansz in the small pinnace *Duyfken*, passed across the western entrance to the island-strewn strait which separates Australia from New Guinea (Flinders, 1814: viii). He thought these lands were connected and formed the west coast of New Guinea. But, as Flinders said: 'Without being conscious of it, the commander of the *Duyfken* made the first authenticated discovery of any part of the great South Land, about the month of March 1606 . . .'

It was less than a year later that Luis Vaes de Torres, the Spanish voyager, sailed through the same strait and as noted by Flinders (1814: x): 'It cannot be doubted, that the "very large islands" seen by

1

Torres, at the 11th degree of south latitude, were the hills of Cape York.'

First Contact with Aborigines

It was the expedition of the Dutch navigator, Jan Carstensz, which made the first recorded contact with Aborigines. In January 1623, the Governor of Java, in what was then the Dutch East Indies, despatched two yachts, the *Pera* and the *Arnhem*, on a voyage to explore the land of 'Nova Guinea'.

On 12th April the party sighted the coast of New Holland. The ships sailed into the Gulf of Carpentaria where landings were made, the latter in the estuary of the Gilbert River. Here they met and clashed with Aborigines. A river, the 'Spult', is shown on old charts in the vicinity of the present Liverpool River. There is also another opening marked the 'Speult', on the eastern side of the Gulf, later named Endeavour Strait by Cook. The vessels finished the voyage and noted the discovery of 'the great islands Arnhem and the Spult'. No journal of the voyage has survived but it is known a party landed on the coast of New Guinea, where Carstensz of the *Arnhem* and eight of his crew, were killed by the natives.

The *Pera* made the last part of the voyage alone. She crossed the head of the Gulf of Carpentaria, following the course of the *Duyfken*, and passing Cape Keer-Weer, continued southward. The report of the voyage was unfavourable, and is summed up in the official despatches of the company: 'In this discovery were found everywhere shallow waters and barren coasts, islands altogether thinly peopled by divers cruel, poor and brutal nations, and of very little use to the Dutch East India Company' (Favenc, 1888: 23-24). Pera Head, in the Gulf, is another memorial of this voyage.

A few years later, in April 1636, Gerrit Tomaz Pool sailed from Banda, in the Moluccas (Indonesia) in the path of Carstensz. Strong easterly winds prevented him from reaching the west coast of New Guinea. He shaped his course almost due south, discovered the coast of Arnhem Land and sailed along its shore for nearly 200 kilometres. Pool sighted many columns of smoke rising from the land but made no contact with Aborigines.

In January, 1644, after his discovery of Van Diemen's Land, Abel Jansz Tasman, sailed from Batavia in the *Limmen* on a second voyage of exploration. He was soon in the Gulf of Carpentaria. As he skirted the coast in a southerly direction he gave names to different coastal features including Limmen Bight, Maria Island and Groote Eylandt (Favenc, 1888: 25-26). He eventually reached the mouth of what is now the McArthur River.

Descriptions of the Aborigines

The first descriptions of the inhabitants of the rather forbidding land emerging in the south were noted by the British privateer William Dampier during his voyage round the world (1698: 463-464). He landed on the north-west coast of Australia in 1688 and was impressed neither with the land nor the Aborigines: 'This part of it that we saw is all low even Land, with sandy Banks against the Sea, only the Points are rocky, and so are some of the Islands in this Bay. The Land is of a dry sandy Soil, destitute of Water, except you make Wells; yet producing divers sorts of Trees . . .

'The inhabitants of this Country are the miserablest People in the world. The *Hodmadods* of *Monamatapa*, though a nasty People, yet for Wealth are Gentlemen to these; who have no Houses and Skin Garments, Sheep, Poultry, and Fruits of the Earth, Ostrich Eggs, etc. as the *Hodmadods* have; and setting aside their humane shape, they differ but little from Brutes. They are tall, strait-bodied, and thin, with small long Limbs. They have great Heads, round Foreheads, and great Brows. Their Eye-lids are always half closed, to keep the Flies out of their Eyes: they being so troublesome here, that no fanning will keep them from coming to ones Face; and without the assistance of both hands to keep them off, they will creep into ones Nostrils; and Mouth too, if the Lips are not shut very close. So that from their Infancy being thus annoyed with these Insects, they do never open their Eyes, as other People: and therefore they cannot see far; unless they hold up their Heads, as if they were looking at somewhat over them.

'They have great Bottle noses, pretty full lips, and wide mouths. The two fore-teeth of their upper Jaw are wanting in all of them, men and women, old and young; whether they draw them out, I know not: Neither have they any Beards. They are long visaged, and of a very unpleasing aspect; having no one graceful feature in their faces. Their Hair is black, short and curl'd, like that of the Negroes: and not long and lank like the common *Indians* . . .'

The outline of the north coast of Australia was beginning to emerge and in 1802 and 1803 Matthew Flinders added a number of new features when he charted the western side of the Gulf of Carpentaria Near the English Company's Islands (named by him) he met a large fleet of Macassan praus engaged in trepang fishing. The leader of the party was named Pobassoo, from whom Flinders learned that there were sixty vessels with a personnel of 1 000 men working along the north coasts. These belonged to the Rajah of Buni. Pobassoo also told of frequent clashes between fishermen and hostile Aborigines.

3

Macassan contact in north Australia has been shown by Macknight (1969: 4) to have extended from the early twentieth century back over more than 350 years. The Aborigines made many records of their visits in the caves of Arnhem Land (Plate 2) and adopted from the regular visitors the dug-out canoe, tobacco pipes (Plate 12 bottom left), iron for tools and weapons, bottle glass for use as scrapers, and possibly sculpture in the round. In addition some Macassarese words were adopted into the vocabulary and local place names are still a reminder of early contacts with the visitors from the north.

Ceremonial and mythological repercussions of Macassan contact were noted in the 1930s by Thomson (1949: 89-90). He found a group on the Glyde River which had come strongly under the influence of the Macassarese and adopted a square-faced bottle as a clan totem. The non-material representation or effigy of the bottle was carved from solid ironwood and painted with a sacred totemic design. This, said Thomson, was a recognition of the economic and spiritual value of glass.

Berndt and Berndt (1954: 61-62) describe burial posts and figures in use in north-west Arnhem Land which were inspired by outside contact.

Discovery of Alligator Rivers

The Alligator Rivers were discovered in 1818 by Phillip Parker King, commander of H.M.S. *Mermaid* and son of the third Governor of New South Wales. At the time of the discovery he was on special survey work in north Australia for the British Admiralty.

In April 1818, King traced the north coast of Arnhem Land. Between the 20th-24th he discovered and explored Port Essington (see map 1). At the entrance to Western Point a wrecked canoe was found and also a discarded spear described by King as '. . . different from any that we had before seen; it was headed with a sharp pointed splinter of quartz, about four inches [10.1 cm] long, and an inch and a half [3.8 cm] broad; the shaft was of the mangrove-tree, seven feet eight inches [2.3 m] long, and appeared, from a small hole at the end, to have been propelled by a throwing-stick; the stone-head was fastened on by a ligature of plaited grass, covered by a mass of gum: it was the most formidable weapon of the sort we had ever yet seen.' (King 1827: 86-87).

Many other traces of Aborigines were found. On one excursion a tree was seen which had been cut down by some sharp instrument. King reasoned that the Aborigines must have obtained iron tools from Macassan fishermen. A shell midden noticed near the beach was described: '. . . a curious mound, constructed entirely of shells,

4

Plate 1 A legendary hero painted on the back wall of a rock shelter located at the base of the escarpment to the south of Lightning Dreaming. The walls of the shelter are unusually rough as the outcrop is composed of conglomerate rock.

Plate 2 Macassan praus feature in many rock painting sites, in particular those near the coast and inlets.

rudely heaped together, measuring thirty feet [9.1 m] in diameter, and fourteen feet [4.2 m] in height . . . and was supposed to be a burying-place of the Indians.'

On leaving the inner harbour King anchored the *Mermaid* in Knocker's Bay on the west side of the port named by him Essington as a tribute to the memory of a close friend, Vice-Admiral Sir William Essington, K.C.B. In the afternoon a party set off to examine an opening in the mangroves at the bottom of the bay. King (1827: 87-89) provides an interesting account of this survey which ended with an exciting encounter with local Aborigines: 'After pulling through its various winding channels for about a mile [1.6 km], where it was scarcely broad enough for the boat to pass, its further investigation was given up, and we commenced our return, but the mangroves were so thick, and formed so impervious a net-work, that we had great difficulty in effecting it. When about half-way towards the

6

Plate 3 Port Essington, a British Settlement established on the north Australian coast from 1838 to 1849.

mouth, we found the boat impeded by the roots of a mangrove bush; whilst the boat's crew was busily employed in clearing the rudder, we were suddenly startled by the shout of a party of Indians, who were concealed from our view by a projecting bush, not more than eight or ten yards [7.3 or 9.1 m] from us: our situation was rather alarming, from the boat being so entangled, and the river not being broad enough for the oars to be used. No sooner had the natives uttered the shout, than they leaped into the water armed with spears and clubs; but the moment they made their appearance around the tree, two muskets loaded with ball, and a fowling-piece with small shot, were fired over their heads, which had the desired effect, for they gave up their premeditated attack, and quickly disappeared among the bushes on the opposite side, where they remained screaming and vociferating loudly in angry threatening voices, whilst we were clearing the boat from the bushes that obstructed our progress.'

Plate 4 The Arnhem Land escarpment stretches for many kilometres in an unbroken line of weathered cliffs. *Top:* The escarpment looking south-west from Hickey (Sawcut) Creek (Lightning Dreaming). The entrance to Deaf Adder Valley can be seen in the middle distance. Explorers Leichhardt and McKinlay were the first Europeans to visit this region. *Bottom:* The spectacular rockface of Mt Brockman is highly significant to living Aborigines. Rock paintings and beeswax designs occur in shelters on the large boulders to the right of the base. Another site exists near the summit of the mount.

The party continued down the creek but was soon assailed by a shower of spears and stones from Aborigines concealed in the mangroves. 'Happily, however', King remarks, 'we received no damage, although the spears and stones fell about us very thickly, and several of the former struck the boat. A volley of musketry was fired into the mangroves, but we could not ascertain whether any of the balls took effect, since we could not see our assailants. A wound from one of their stone-headed weapons, from our want of surgical knowledge, must in such a climate have proved fatal, and we considered our escape truly providential. As soon as we were out of reach of their spears, which they continued to throw until it was of no use, we hoisted the sail, and steered round the shores of the bay. We had not proceeded far, before their canoe was observed secured to the beach by a small rope, which offered so good an opportunity of punishing these savages for their treacherous attack, that we landed and brought it away; and upon examining its contents, we found not only their clubs, but also a large quantity of bivalve shell-fish . . . and three very formidable clubs . . . The canoe was nearly new, it measured eighteen feet [5.4 m] in length, and two [61 cm] in breadth, and would easily carry eight persons; the sides were supported by two poles fastened to the gunwale by strips of a climbing plant (*flagellaria indica*), that grows abundantly hereabouts, and with which also the ends of the canoe were neatly, and even tastefully joined; the poles were spanned together on either side by rope constructed of strips of bark. The canoe was made of one sheet of bark, but in the bottom, within it, short pieces were placed cross-ways, in order to preserve its shape, and increase its strength.'

Early on the following morning the *Mermaid* sailed out of Port Essington and passed around its western head. As it entered the bay a Macassan encampment was seen on the beach. There were several praus at anchor close by; other boats were at anchor on the western shore, close to the encampment. King anchored his ship about three kilometres from them.

Soon afterwards a canoe was sent out from the praus and after some persuasion it came alongside. King (1827: 94) describes the event in some detail: 'The canoe was fitted for fishing, it was paddled by a man and five boys, and was steered by a younger man, who from his dress and authority, appeared to be of some consequence amongst them. During their visit their curiosity was much excited by everything they saw; and, having drunk pretty freely of our port wine, they talked incessantly. They remained with us three hours, during the greater part of which their canoe was absent catching fish. One of our visitors was very communicative, and by means of signs and a

9

few words of the Malay language, which we understood, he explained that their Rajah's proa was armed with two small guns, and carried a compass. On looking at our binnacle, they pointed to the north-west rhumb, and made us easily understand that it was the course they always steered on their return to Macassar.

'Upon mentioning the natives of the coast, and showing them the stone-headed spear that we had found, they evinced their dislike to them very plainly—they called them "Maregas", Maregas being, as we afterwards found, their appelation of this part of the coast.'

On 6th May, King discovered the entrance to the East Alligator River which he explored for a distance of several kilometres. He found the country low, dreary and flat, covered in mangroves which were the habitat of vast numbers of water birds. He saw no Aborigines but noted their fires burning in all directions.

As he continued along the coast King discovered and named Barron and Field Islands. He then entered the mouth of the South Alligator River which he navigated for a distance of fifty-eight kilometres, noting that alligators '. . . were as numerous as in the other river, whence the name of Alligator Rivers was bestowed upon them' (King 1827: 100-104).

Reports of great rivers entering the sea on the north coast of Australia led to proposals for a settlement. At the end of 1823 William Barns, a trader for twenty years in the East Indies, suggested to the Colonial Department, London, that a trading post should be established. At that time, there were no British possessions in the East India trade and the Dutch had shut their ports to British shipping. Barns emphasised the value of the trade in trepang caught by Macassans in north Australian waters and postulated that a British settlement would offset trade advantages obtained by the Dutch territories.

Attempts to Establish British Settlements

The plan for a trading post was adopted and in 1824 James Bremer, in command of H.M.S. *Tamar*, set sail from England for New South Wales with instructions from the Admiralty to found a colony in the north. Bremer reached Port Essington via Sydney on 20th September, 1824. He landed and hoisted the British flag in an act of formal possession. However, on failing to find fresh-water he was forced to move to Melville Island where he anchored a few days later.

Bremer and his party established a small settlement which they named Fort Dundas. This 'outpost of Empire' struggled on for but a short period. After two years the Commander, Major Campbell, was compelled to report the disadvantages of Fort Dundas to the Governor at Sydney. The Colonial Office in the same year decided to found a new settlement at Raffles Bay, twenty kilometres to the east of Port Essington. Meanwhile at Fort Dundas relations with the Aborigines declined rapidly, reaching a crisis in November 1827 when the Assistant Colonial Surgeon, John Gold and John Green, Commissary Storekeeper, were killed while taking an evening walk in the bush.

Responsibility for founding the new settlement at Raffles Bay was given to James Stirling who, in H.M.S. *Success* accompanied by three transports, was sent in May 1827 from Sydney to northern waters. On board was a detachment of the 39th Regiment, under Captain Smyth, and a number of convicts. Stirling reached Raffles Bay on 19th June and established a settlement on the eastern side of the bay, close to some fresh-water lagoons. It was not until the following year that personnel was moved from Fort Dundas to Raffles Bay.

The life of this settlement was also to be short and Raffles Bay was abandoned on 29th August, 1830, in favour of a new settlement in the temperate latitude of Western Australia where in 1828 Stirling had found a favourable site on the Swan River.

With all its disadvantages Raffles Bay had a measure of success as was outlined in a report to Sir Gordon Bremer for the period March-May 1829. There was some indication of the settlement becoming an important trading post between the military authorities and the Macassan trepangers. Thirty-four praus manned by 1056 fishermen, had visited Raffles Bay during that particular three month period.

Despite initial favourable reports, the problems which beset the Fort Dundas settlement on Melville Island applied also to Raffles Bay. There had been frequent attacks on the garrison by Aborigines, much sickness and many deaths. Captain Collett Barker, one of the commanders, is said to have had many difficulties to contend with, in implementing his policy of humane treatment for Aborigines. 'No other individual in the settlement could be brought to consider these "poor beings" in any other light than wild beasts. Those who had to work in the bush, conscious, perhaps, of their own conduct, were occasionally under great alarm, not being entrusted with fire-arms. Several times they were frightened, but never received any injury, the natives wishing to be on friendly terms.' (Wilson 1835: 74).

Shortly after Barker's arrival, the Aborigines '. . . since an unfortunate affair at Bowen's Straits had kept out of sight, again made an appearance in the vicinity of the settlement. Barker used every endeavour to induce them to enter the camp, apparently without success, until a child, belonging to one of the soldiers, went and led the Chief, Wellington, by the hand.' According to contemporary reports, he '. . . was evidently under great alarm, looking back frequently, and

11

addressing himself to Waterloo, his *fidus Achates*, who kept in his rear.

'But at length, gathering confidence, and relying on the faith of the strangers, he ventured in, when he was treated with much kindness, and departed apparently highly pleased.'

Paradoxically, in 1831, while on the return journey to Sydney, Barker was speared by Aborigines while exploring the mouth of the River Murray in South Australia, discovered by a brother officer, Captain Charles Sturt, during his epic journey of discovery down the Murray River in 1829-1830.

Despite the disappointing attempts to colonise the north of Australia, the British Government persisted with plans for a settlement. Attention was focussed again on the area in 1837 when there were strong rumours that the French were preparing an expedition to the north coast. Sir Gordon Bremer again was charged with the task of founding a British post. He left Sydney on 17th September, 1838, on H.M.S. *Alligator*, in company with two other ships. Cape York was reached on 20th October and there Bremer landed and formally took possession of the territory. The ships sailed into Port Essington six days later and began establishment of the settlement of Victoria.

On 1st May, his Lieutenant, P. B. Stewart, accompanied by two men, all of them armed for fear of attack by Aborigines, set out on what was perhaps the most ambitious land exploration carried out in north Australia to that time. With provisions for seven days carried on two Timor ponies, they explored the surrounding country. They were impressed with the fertility of the soil and the abundance of running water and were surprised to find the Aborigines extremely friendly and of great assistance in guiding the party through dense undergrowth.

Interest in charting the north coast continued in earnest in 1839 when J. C. Wickham, in the sloop *Beagle*, continued the survey begun in 1818 by Phillip Parker King. The Adelaide River was discovered and Port Darwin named. It is interesting to note that during their stay the crew noticed that an epidemic of influenza was raging among the Aborigines who had been friendly with white men.

By 1840 the survey of the north coastline was well advanced but British settlement was still tenuous. It was in 1845 when Dr Ludwig

13

Leichhardt arrived at Port Essington (Plate 3) after an epic fifteen month journey from Moreton Bay (Brisbane), that knowledge of the hinterland was expanded.

Land Exploration

In mid-November, 1845, Leichhardt stood on the edge of the Arnhem Land escarpment in the Deaf Adder-Jim Jim Creek area. He was the first non-Aboriginal to look out over the vast Alligator Rivers Region. He noted the steep, rugged escarpment, the forest lands and beyond them the wet lands and plains cut by rivers winding their way towards the north coast.

After finding a way down the precipitous escarpment Leichhardt and his party worked their way through the wet lands of Nourlangie and Magela Creeks to the East Alligator River. He comments on the residual outliers of the Arnhem Land Plateau in the general area of Cannon Hill which he describes as: '. . . conical and strange-shaped hills, either isolated or connected in short ranges; and when we came to the higher part of the river, rocky sandstone ranges, rising abruptly out of the level of the plain, appeared to surround the valley of the river. At the foot of these rocky ranges fine lagoons were found, which were so crowded with wild geese that Brown, one of my black fellows, shot six at one shot.'

Leichhardt (1846: 46-48) describes further the country: 'The valley of the Upper East Alligator, which I should rather call Goose River (for nowhere we observed so many geese—and what is called alligator is no alligator but a crocodile) is one of the most romantic spots I have seen in my wanderings. A broad valley, level, with the most luxuriant verdure, abrupt hills and ranges rising everywhere along its east and west sides, and closing it apparently at its southern extremity; lagoons, forming fine sheets of water, scattered over it; a creek, though with salt water, winding through it.

'After having crossed the river I went to the northwards, passed a plain about eight miles [12.8 km] long, from which I saw bluff mountain heads to the north-east, which seemed to indicate the valley of a northerly river, entered the forest land, passed several creeks, running to the eastward and followed a well-trodden footpath of the natives, which led me through rock sandstone ridges, over numerous creeks running to the westward to the broad sandy bed of a river, with fine pools of water, which I consider to be the fresh-water branch of the East Alligator [Cooper Creek], coming from the east. Not very far from the river, we came to a fine lagoon, beyond which a large plain extended.

14

'I passed the plain, and entered the forest land. Just where the latter commenced, on a swampy ground between sandstone rocks, the first tracks of buffaloes were observed . . . we travelled in a northerly course again, through forest land, and crossed a small plain, in which a mangrove creek turned to the westward, and further on a tea-tree swamp equally to the west. On a fine plain we met a tribe of black fellows (Nywall's tribe), who guided us to a good-sized lagoon. This plain extended far to the northward and westward. Two isolated peaks and two low ranges were seen from it to the east and south-east. We crossed and skirted these plains in a north-north-west course, and entered the forest land, which was undulating with low ironstone ridges, from which numerous creeks went down to Van Diemen's Gulf, along which we travelled. Black fellows had guided us two days, but they left us at the neck of the Cobourg Peninsula, which we entered on a fine footpath. Keeping a little too much to the northward on a narrow neck, we came to westerly waters and to Mountnorris Bay.

'I turned, however, again to the westward, to come to westerly waters. Creeks are numerous on both sides, and fresh water was frequent after the late thunder showers. Keeping a little too much to the northward, from the latter creek, I came to Raffle's Bay, from which black fellows familiar with the settlement guided us round Port Essington to Victoria, which I entered at about five o'clock, the 17th December, 1845.'

Interesting observations were made by Leichhardt (1846: 49) on the prevalence of buffalo already at large in Arnhem Land at that time: 'The tracks of buffaloes became more and more numerous as we advanced on the neck of the Peninsula. They formed at last a regular broad path along the sea coast, sometimes skirting the mangrove swamps, in which all the western and eastern creeks end, sometimes entering into the swamp itself. Farther on other paths turned off into the forest and along creeks, and formed a network which rendered it impossible for me to keep to the principal black fellow's footpath, leading from Nywall's lagoon to the settlement. We frequently saw buffaloes as we went on . . . in riding along it I saw three or four at the time hurrying out of the deep holes of water within the creek to which they came in the heat of the day to cool themselves . . . the buffaloes are equally abundant between Raffle's Bay and the harbour; and the whole country, particularly round the Baki Baki Bay and on the neck, is as closely covered with buffalo tracks as a well-stocked cattle run of New South Wales could be.'

Leichhardt's (1847: 486) encounters with the Aborigines were numerous. As he descended the escarpment into the Alligator Rivers Region he met several Aborigines who came up to exchange presents:

15

'Four natives came to our camp; they made us presents of red ochre, which they seemed to value highly, of a spear and a spear's head made of baked sandstone. In return I gave them a few nails, and as I was under the necessity of parting with everything heavy . . . I also gave them my geological hammer.'

A large group of Aborigines was met at the commencement of the plain. Leichhardt continues: 'They were armed with small goose spears, and with flat "wommalas"; but, although they were extremely noisy, they did not show the slightest hostile intention. One of them had a shawl and neckerchief of English manufacture: and another carried an iron tomahawk, which he said he got from north-west by north. They knew Pichenclumbo (Van Diemen's Gulf), and pointed to the north-west by north, when we asked for it. I made them various presents: and they gave us some of their ornaments and bunches of goose feathers in return, but shewed the greatest reluctance in parting with their throwing sticks (Wommalas). They were inclined to theft, and I had to mount Brown on horseback to keep them out of our camp.'

On the next day the Aborigines returned to the camp very early in the morning, and took an intense interest in what the party was eating, but would not taste anything offered to them. As the party moved on Leichhardt (1847: 493) remarks in his journal: 'The natives were very numerous, employing themselves either in fishing or burning grass on the plains, or digging for roots. I saw here a noble fig-tree, under the shade of which seemed to have been the camping place of the natives for the last century. It was growing at the place where we first came to the broadest outlet of the swamp.'

Leichhardt found it difficult to communicate with Aborigines. On one occasion, as he crossed an extensive swamp, he recorded the event in some detail (1847: 494-495): 'Several times I wished to communicate with the natives who followed us, but every time I turned my horse's head, they ran away; however, finding my difficulties increased, whilst attempting to cross the swamp, I dismounted and walked up to one of them, and taking his hand, gave him a sheet of paper on which I wrote some words, giving him to understand, as well as I could, that he had nothing to fear as long as he carried the paper. By this means I induced him to walk with me, but considerably in advance of my train . . . he kept manfully near me, and pointed out

the sounder parts of the swamp, until we came to a large pool, on which were a great number of geese, when he gave me to understand that he wished Brown to go and shoot them; for these natives, as well as those who visited us last night, were well acquainted with the effects of fire arms.

'We encamped at this pool, and the natives flocked round us from every direction. Boys of every age, lads, young men and old men too, came, every one armed with his bundle of goose spears, and his throwing sticks. They observed, with curious eye, everything we did, and made long explanations to each other of the various objects presented to their gaze. Our eating, drinking, dress, skin, combing, boiling, our blankets, straps, horses, everything, in short, was new to them, and was earnestly discussed, particularly by one of the old men, who amused us with his drollery and good humour in trying to persuade each of us to give him something. They continually used the words "Perikot, Nōkot, Mankiterre, Lumbo Lumbo, Nana Nana Nana," all of which we did not understand till after our arrival at Port Essington, where we learned that they meant "very good, no good, Malays very far."

'Our good friends, the natives, were with us again very early in the morning; they approached us in long file, incessantly repeating the words above mentioned . . . which they seemed to consider a kind of introduction. After having guided us over the remaining part of the swamp to the firm land, during which they gave us the most evident proof of their skill in spearing geese—they took their leave of us.'

In the East Alligator area, Leichhardt '. . . observed a great number of long conical fish and crab traps at the crossing place in the creek and in many of the tributary salt-water channels. They were made apparently of *flagellaria* . . . seven other natives visited us again in the morning . . . [one] carried a little pointed stick, and a flat piece of wood with a hole in it, for the purpose of obtaining fire . . . The old camps of the natives, which we passed in the forest, were strewed with the shells of goose eggs, which shewed what an important article these birds formed in the culinary department of the natives; and, whilst their meat and eggs served them for food, their feathers afforded them a protection against the flies which swarmed round their bodies during the day.' (Leichhardt 1847: 513-516).

19

Plate 8 The main rock shelter on Inyalak Hill near Oenpelli. The site has been declared a Prescribed Area to ensure protection of the rich body art on the walls and ceiling of this large dry shelter.

Leichhardt's journey through the Alligator Rivers Region was the beginning of a new era for the Aborigines who had made it their home for many thousands of years. The Macassan fisherman had been content to visit the coast and return home again each year; the new intruders would eventually move in to stay.

It was the British Government, through its colony in New South Wales, that initiated and brought to near completion, exploration of the north Australian coastline. But it was the explorations planned in Adelaide that expanded knowledge of north Australia and led to colonisation.

Northern Territory Annexed to South Australia

The opening of the north to pastoralists followed quickly in the wake of John McDouall Stuart's adventurous cross-continent journey from Adelaide to the Gulf of Carpentaria in 1862.

On 6th July, 1863, the Northern Territory was annexed to South Australia. The Government, anxious to exploit the resources of its newly acquired Territory, appointed the first Government Resident, Colonel B. T. Finnis, a pioneer South Australian, on 3rd March, 1864. A settlement was established at Escape Cliffs by the end of August of the same year.

There was dissatisfaction with the initial progress made at the settlement and the Government, in its bid to extend knowledge of the tropical north, appointed John McKinlay to carry out a thorough land exploration and report on the best sites for settlements and the most suitable localities for a capital.

McKinlay arrived at Escape Cliffs on 5th November, 1865. After making the necessary preparations he left on his explorations on 14th January, 1866. Prior to departure he recorded his assessment of Escape Cliffs: 'A greater scene of desolation and waste could not be pictured . . . as a seaport and city this place is worthless.' (McKinlay, S.A.P.P., No. 131, 1866: 1).

McKinlay arranged for stores to be left at Roper and Liverpool Rivers which he hoped to reach by the beginning of April. A rendezvous was planned with Captain F. Howard of the South Australian Surveying Schooner *Beatrice* which had arrived at Escape Cliffs on a marine survey of north Australia on 28th December, 1865.

McKinlay set off inland along the general line of the Adelaide River. He later turned east and made his way to the escarpment along which he travelled for several weeks. By the end of March he was imprisoned by the monsoonal wet season in a small area of country on one of the branches of the Alligator River. Stretches of vast swamps, lines of precipitous cliffs and wild, broken, sandstone offered McKinlay no avenue of escape. Many of his horses died and food supplies became almost exhausted. As he could neither go forward nor retreat, McKinlay decided to construct a raft and float down the East Alligator River, in a valiant attempt to return to Escape Cliffs by water. The remaining horses were killed one by one, their flesh cut into strips and their hides utilised to build what must have been one of the strangest crafts ever put together in Australia.

On 29th June, at the precise moment when the party was to embark on their makeshift boat called *Pioneer*, they were attacked by Aborigines who, until then, had appeared to be friendly. However, this

Plate 9 Nimbuwah rises dramatically out of the alluvial plain some 32km to the north-east of Oenpelli. This 214m high feature is a sacred site with important legendary significance to Aborigines. Cooper Creek flows nearby on its passage north from Nabarlek.

scare over, with no resultant casualties, all hands launched the boat and a start downstream was made on the ebb tide from a point about six kilometres north of Cannon Hill. On 2nd July the open sea was reached and the *Pioneer* was worked across the mouth of the South Alligator River. On 5th July, they reached Escape Cliffs. (S.A.P.P., No. 131, 1866: 1-21).

Meanwhile the *Beatrice* had sailed from Adam Bay on 28th January, arriving in Mountnorris Bay two days later. Survey operations were commenced and continued, whenever the weather would allow, until 10th March, by which time the main coastline had been examined from Bowen Straits (Croker Island) to Port Brogden (see Map 1). Howard found the Aborigines of the area very friendly; several spoke English, and remembered the names of people at Port Essington.

During their stay at Mountnorris Bay two Macassan praus anchored near Copeland Island: 'The Malays put up their curing-house and boilers and commenced their fishing for trepang at once. Each proa had about fifteen fishing-boats, manned by a crew of six or seven men, one or two of whom were generally Australian natives. The Malays seemed a quiet set of people and took little notice of us. The proas hoisted Dutch colours when first we approached.' (S.A.P.P., No. 79, 1866: 1).

Howard noted the presence of buffaloes in large numbers and was the first to record the occurrence of pigs on Cobourg Peninsula. Some of his men who were lost for a time in the bush also saw a pony.

After leaving Mountnorris Bay the *Beatrice* followed the coast eastwards. Numerous Macassan fishing praus were seen off the east side of Goulburn Island and in the bays to the eastward. Off Cape Cuthbert several praus under Dutch colours were encountered running to the westward.

The *Beatrice* arrived in the Liverpool River on 25th March and Howard and his party took the schooner upstream into fresh water, proceeding as far as they could in the boats. Howard learnt later from Aborigines at the East Alligator River that McKinlay and his party had floated down the river and along the coast. The *Beatrice* arrived back at Escape Cliffs twenty-six days after the safe arrival of McKinlay on his strange life-raft.

McKinlay and Howard were followed by other explorers in rapid succession as the South Australian Government was determined to carry out, as quickly as possible, a detailed survey of the north to assess its potential for settlement.

In 1867, Francis W. Cadell of River Murray navigation fame, led the Northern Territory Exploration Expedition. The object was to examine the Liverpool River area as a prospective site for a capital. Cadell arrived off the Liverpool River in May and proceeded to explore the hinterland, noting that the Aborigines were numerous and made large fires to attract their attention. It is interesting that Cadell also records in his journal the sighting of a Macassan prau: 'Whilst steaming up against a strong monsoon, a little after daylight, a proa, flying before the wind, ran past us, under Dutch colours. She is apparently the last of the fleet, and making the most of her way home. Working to the eastward all this day, the natives on the Goulburn Islands making many signals to us.' (Cadell, S.A.P.P., No. 178, 1868: 2). Cadell reported favourably on the region but the Government was not convinced and in December, 1868, the South Australian Surveyor-General, G. W. Goyder was sent to complete the long delayed survey. He chose the eastern side of Port Darwin as the ideal site for a capital in the north and named it Palmerston.

There are few written records of the reactions of Aborigines to the first contacts with the new culture. The many ochre paintings in the galleries of the Alligator Rivers Region which depict sailing vessels (Plate 12), men, guns, pistols, axes and introduced stock, leave no doubt that the movements of the new intruders, like those of the Macassarese before them, were being carefully watched and noted down in the form of paintings in the age-old galleries of the region.

Exploitation of Natural Resources

With a site for a capital chosen there was a spate of both official and private exploration and survey work. The north was ripe for exploitation. Emphasis was initially on pastoral development. Buffaloes, brought to Port Essington, had been let loose on the abandonment of the settlement. Freedom from disease and immunity from attack by other animals enabled the buffalo to increase at a remarkable rate and freelance hunters were quick to exploit the large herds that had built up on the vast coastal plains.

The initial success was short-lived due to innumerable problems and in the years 1890, 1894 and 1898 some 200 000 km² of country were surrendered in the vicinity of the McArthur, Roper and Alligator Rivers and on Cobourg Peninsula. In 1893 the 150 000 km² *Florida* run in Arnhem Land was relinquished. Pastoralists had begun to realise that there were great difficulties attending the establishment of cattle runs in the monsoonal lands of the north (Duncan 1967: 46).

As early as 1869, the search for minerals had begun in the hope of rapid monetary returns. There were small strikes of gold, copper, silver, lead and tin; an export industry was quick to develop.

The discovery of gold at Pine Creek in the 1880s gave rise to great optimism and a railway was constructed from Darwin to Pine Creek, largely by Chinese labourers, between 1887 and 1889, to service expanding mining activities. Paintings at a site in the Cooper Creek region were said by Aborigines to depict the construction of this railway (Plate 12 bottom right). The economics of mineral exploitation in the north were not to be really viable until there was a demand for a new range of minerals such as iron ore, bauxite and uranium. (Conigrave 1936: 186).

Relations with Aborigines

Increased land exploitation and settlement, was to bring drastic changes for the Aborigines of north Australia. As early as 1869, Goyder (S.A.P.P., No. 157, 1869: 2), when commenting on the killing of two of his party by Aborigines, wrote with considerable insight and feeling: 'I had also to bear in mind that we were in what to them appeared unauthorised and unwarrantable occupation of their country, and where territorial rights are so strictly observed by the natives, that even a chief of one tribe will neither hunt upon nor remove anything from the territory of another without first obtaining permission.'

By 1884 a serious situation was developing between pastoralists, miners and Aborigines. The Government Resident in Darwin, J. Langdon Parsons, wrote of the problems in the following terms: 'I fear unquiet times may be expected in connection with the native tribes. The blacks are beginning to realize that the white man, with his herds, and his fences, and his preservation of water, is interfering with what they properly enough, from their point of view, regard as their natural right. Their hunting grounds and game preserves are being disturbed, and their food supply both diminished and rendered uncertain.

'They can no longer, as they could a few years ago, travel from one lagoon or billabong to another, and be certain that on arrival there would be flocks of wild fowl to be snared. Nor can they, as of old, when they desired a repast of snakes, iguanas, or other reptiles, set fire to the first piece of well-grassed country they encounter. The stockholder uses the billabong for his cattle, and wild fowl are scared away; he wants the grass for his cattle and very vigorously lets the blackfellows understand that it is at their peril they put the firestick to it. Naturally out of these conditions conflict arises and will continue. The natives will resist the intrusion of the whites and regard themselves as robbed of their inheritance; they will set the grass alight when they are so minded, and, if hungry, or by way of reprisal, they will spear cattle when they think they are out of the range of the rifle. How to deal equitably with these Aboriginals—how, while facilitating the settlement and stocking of the country by Europeans, at the same time to atone for what is an undoubted loss of food supply in consequence to the natives, is a problem much easier to state than to solve. That settlement and stocking must and will go on is certain —that outrages will be committed by both sides is probable; but even those who do not claim to be philanthropists are not satisfied with the contemplation that the blacks are to be removed off the face of the earth.

'It appears to me that reserves but imperfectly meet the case—though large reserves ought, I think to be proclaimed—because the native life is essentially nomadic, and because of imperious demands of hunger take him where the water-lily roots, yams and game are to be found. Serious and unhappy conflicts can only be avoided by a strong sense of justice and consideration for the natives on the part of the Europeans, and probably not even then.

'This subject has been forced upon public attention by the recent outrages on the Daly River and at Argument Flat. It is still more deeply impressed upon me by the intelligence which reaches me from station managers and drovers. At the Katherine, Elsey, and Newcastle Waters, difficulties have arisen in connection with blacks and cattle. Mr Lindsay Crawford states that on the Victoria the blacks are daring and defiant; Mr Creaghe states that at the Limmen River they are spearing his cattle, and that he must take measures to prevent recurrence; Mr Hay states much the same condition of things as existing on the Roper, where one or two natives have firearms.

'The arrival of the force of black trackers will give us a very valuable adjunct to the police force in bringing offenders to justice, but no numbers of trackers or of police that could be organised can prevent outrages over the immense area of country which is now being stocked.

'At present I can but state the difficulties, and do the best as circumstances arise.

'No doubt, so far as the Daly natives are concerned, the conviction of four of their number after trial, and their execution near the scene where the murders were committed, will have a wholesome deterrent effect; but beyond the region occupied by the tribes who frequent the river, little or nothing of it will be known.' (S.A.P.P., No. 53, 1885: 10).

Formation of Aboriginal Settlement at Oenpelli

Among the adventurous hunters attracted to Arnhem Land by reports of large numbers of wild buffalo was well-known Territorian, Paddy Cahill. In the 1880s he commenced shooting in the swampy plains of the Alligator Rivers Region where large herds prospered on the vast grasslands of the black soil plains.

Cahill made excursions into the region each year and was quick to establish friendly contact with the *Kakadu* people who assisted him in the hunt. His intimate knowledge of these people, and the fact that he learnt to speak their language, is said to have won their complete confidence. Eventually Cahill took out a pastoral lease for the area, and in 1906 moved from Delamere Station, south-west of Katherine with horses and cattle, and established a dairy, orchard and garden in the vicinity of where Oenpelli is today. The *Kakadu* settled with

Cahill at Oenpelli where they assisted in the establishment of the property.

The locality, described at the time as being one of great natural beauty, was at the eastern limit of the sub-coastal black-soil plains and about five kilometres from the Spencer Range which is the beginning of the Arnhem Land Plateau. Three hills called Inyalak, Arrkuluk and Nimbabirr, overlook the area. These hills are important totemic sites to local Aborigines as will be detailed later in this report.

A visitor to 'Oenpelli' in 1915 (Masson 1915: 102-113) left on record a description of the settlement and its inhabitants: 'Paddy Cahill . . . still lives on the Alligator, and acts as protector to the aborigines of the district. The banks of the river teem with wild-fowl, so the blacks have never lacked food, and are, in consequence, a fine race of strong, muscular men and pretty, plump lubras. No Chinese are settled there to demoralise them with grog and opium. Here is the Australian aboriginal unspoilt, morally and physically, and here, if anywhere, is the chance of civilising him successfully.

'Paddy Cahill is beginning in the right way. The men are learning to grow vegetables and to build houses of simple design, the lubras are being trained in domestic work, and in due time a school will be established, where the children will be taught reading and writing. But the secret of Paddy Cahill's success lies in his unbounded influence over the natives and in his wonderful sympathy with their customs and beliefs. He never laughs at them; he speaks to them in their own language, and calls them by their native names. In return, they give him their confidence, and no ceremony is too sacred to be enacted before him. Those who work on the homestead are well cared for, induced to be clean, and doctored if they are ill. Their relations with Paddy Cahill are of the friendliest, and yet, though they laugh and joke together, there is never a tinge of insolence on the part of the blacks. You feel that here they have found a true friend and protector—one who, while not discarding their ways, will lead them gradually to his own.

'Paddy Cahill's station, Oenpelli, is truly isolated. To the west his nearest neighbour is reached after a journey of four days overland by horse, at Burrundie, a small siding on the railway line; to the east there is no one between him and the Arafura Sea. Every six weeks or so, Romula, a faithful black henchman, rides into Burrundie and back with mails, or else Paddy Cahill himself sails down the river in his lugger and round the coast to Darwin. This is in the dry season; in the wet, the track is often impassable and storms make the sea journey dangerous, so that the dwellers at Oenpelli are sometimes for six months without a mail.'

Masson set out from Darwin to visit Oenpelli in the steamer *Stuart*, of 280 tons. The ultimate destination was the Roper River in the Gulf of Carpentaria, but on the way she was to call at the East Alligator River, to land, near Oenpelli, a party of surveyors who were to make the first survey of the country. '. . . On the second day out she made her way towards a blank space in the close line of mangroves, the mouth of the [East] Alligator River. Twelve miles [19.3 km] up the river she dropped anchor, and the cruise was continued in a motor-boat towing a punt and a dinghy. We all hoped to find Oenpelli that night, but where to find it was another matter. We knew the station was not situated right on the banks of the river; but how far up it was, where to find the track that led to it, not one of the party had any idea . . .

'For miles and miles we saw nothing but mangroves, grey mud, wild-fowl, and alligators. The alligators, which lay sunning themselves on long spits of mud were of all sizes, from a baby of two or three feet [60.8 or 91.2 cm], like a gigantic lizard that wriggled wildly down the bank at our approach, to a huge twenty-foot [6 m] monster that slowly launched himself into the river, lifted a wicked, grinning old face for an instant above the water, and then vanished swiftly and suddenly.

'The wild-fowl swarmed. Cockatoos hung on the mangroves like large white blossoms; elegant cranes posed daintily on the grey mud; ducks and geese flew in wavy lines across the river; once a flock of turkeys flapped over our heads. But of human habitation the only trace we saw was one native dug-out canoe, laying empty close in to shore . . .

'At last there appeared ahead two fuzzy cone-shaped hills, which, as we approached turned out to be formed of big rocks piled on each other, with jungle growing in the clefts. There were two or three of these strange cones, scattered over a yellow plain, where a few pandanus palms grew in sketchy clumps. Here we stopped to reconnoitre, and hit upon a strange discovery. We climbed up a cleft between two rocks through a tangle of creeper, crawled on our hands and knees up a dark tunnel, with little bats softly hitting our faces, and emerged on a sunny platform, surrounded by great rocks and smelling sweetly of spinifex. The underside of one of these was covered with crude images in red, yellow and white clay. It was a native picture gallery we had discovered. For the most part the paintings seemed to be of birds and fishes, but here and there was an unmistakable alligator or a human form; and scattered amongst them all was the imprint of a red hand. We longed for some one learned in black lore to tell us if the paintings were old, or lately made. The place, so silent, remote, and smelling sweetly, gave the impression that it had been a sacred spot for long ages, and that not one man but the artists of many generations had come there alone to spend sunny hours, lying on their backs below the rock and daubing it with their coloured clays.'

Masson records that they continued the journey, the river gradually narrowing and the everlasting mangroves giving way to thicker, more varied undergrowth. Wide plains, covered with long, golden grass, spread away from each bank. Unable to find the settlement, they camped on the banks of the East Alligator River where they spent a cold and uncomfortable night. Next morning the journey up river was continued.

'This time it was not for long. The wall of rock loomed nearer until at last we were abreast of it, and there on the bank lay a native dug-out and three rough stakes stuck in the mud. This was good enough to be called a jetty. We landed and found to our joy wheel tracks running out to the rocky mountain. While some of the party set out to follow these, the rest of us set fire to the plain. The smoke rushed up into the sky and signalled "white man" to a native camp that was hidden from our eyes. Before long we saw four natives stepping over the plain to meet us—wild, unkempt, unkept, unclad creatures, but most welcome to our eyes . . .' One of the Aborigines stood apart '. . . somewhat morosely, but was distinctly offended when a tactless white asked if he were a myall, or wild black that had not yet come into contact with civilized man. "Me no more myall fella", he said indignantly. As he was smeared from head to foot with wood ash, wore his hair in a high fuzz round his face, and was clad only in a girdle of native string, there was some excuse for the supposition . . . two of his companions, Governor and Charlie, were quite loquacious and admitted with proud chuckles having been in Darwin gaol. From them we learned to our satisfaction that the canoe and the stakes were indeed Cahill's own jetty, and that the wheel tracks ran straight out to Oenpelli.'

The party of three that had set off to follow the waggon tracks had arrived, after eleven kilometres walk, at Paddy Cahill's station. 'The sudden appearance there of three white men, actually on foot, and with no sign of pack horse, caused much excitement. The blacks rushed up to the house calling "Ballanda, Ballanda"—white man— and the Boss and Missis ran out to welcome the strangers. In a short while Romula was despatched with a note to the rest of us waiting anxiously on the river bank. A few wild blacks had collected round us, and presently one pointed to an object moving towards us in the distance—a black-boy on horseback. As he approached the edge of the creek, that wound across the plain, one of the wild blacks suddenly threw up his arms. Romula stopped dead, while the blackfellow

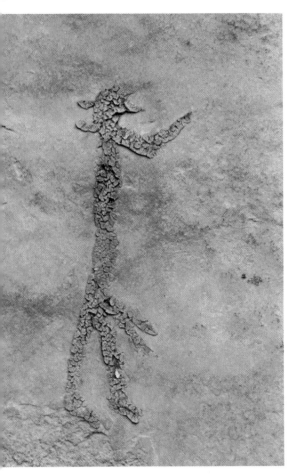

Plate 11 Unique beeswax anthropomorphs were formed by pressing pieces of kneaded beeswax on to the rock surface. *Left:* A male figure with kangaroo head at a site in the Upper Cooper Creek Region. *Right:* A female figure with kangaroo head.

plunged into the jungle bordering the stream and vanished. Some little bit of tribal law this must have been that forbade them to meet face to face. This bit of by-play, so swiftly passed, seemed strangely full of meaning. It seemed to show that the well-clad rider, the trusted friend of white man, was not in reality living in the same world as ourselves, but in one shared by the naked, ash-smeared savage before him—a world swayed by the thoughts and beliefs of a vanished age.

'Romula's note told us that Paddy Cahill and his family were close behind, and by sunset the cavalcade had arrived to welcome the new-comers, and especially the one white woman, the first seen by the women of Oenpelli, Mrs Cahill and her niece, for three years. By

31

nightfall our fires lit up more white faces than had ever before been seen together on the banks of the river, while outside the circle a whole tribe of natives—men, lubras and piccaninnies—kept up a shrill chatter, discussing endlessly the coming of the strangers to the Alligator River.'

Commonwealth Control

By the turn of the century hopes for rapid and prosperous settlement in the Northern Territory had dwindled. Year by year the accumulated debt increased and though there was support in South Australia for retention of the Territory, no sooner had the Commonwealth Government come into being than agitation began for transfer to Federal control. The first step was taken in 1906; the administration finally passed from South Australia to the Commonwealth Government in 1911.

In 1916 the new Administration purchased Paddy Cahill's enterprise at Oenpelli for use as a Government agriculture and experimental station. Moderately successful attempts were made to produce butter for the Darwin market. The Aborigines provided a reasonably stable, though apparently not very efficient, supply of labour. It is interesting that the first shipment of butter to Darwin was boycotted by the unions because it had been made with Aboriginal labour (Simpson 1951: 212). The project was abandoned about 1919.

Attempts were made also to grow cotton. Fields were ploughed and planted but insect pests caused such havoc that this scheme also had to be brought to abrupt termination. Stray plants of introduced cotton are found still in this area; it was used by Aborigines as an alternative to native kapok for ceremonial decorations.

In 1920 a number of small Aboriginal Reserves were proclaimed in the Northern Territory. Included among them was one of 5 180 km² which took in Oenpelli. The proclamation defined the area of the Reserve as commencing at a point on the right bank of the East Alligator River about twenty-three kilometres above Cahill's Crossing thence sixty-four kilometres east, thence sixty-four kilometres north, thence west to the sea coast and south-westerly and south-easterly along the sea coast and the right bank of the East Alligator River (Cole 1972: 48-51).

Several religious bodies were approached to accept responsibility for the Reserve. The Roman Catholic and Methodist missions declined but at the instigation of the Bishop of Carpentaria, Oenpelli was accepted by the Church Missionary Society on 1st June, 1925. It was decided also that the New South Wales Branch of the Church Missionary Society should be responsible for its administration, while the remainder of the 5 180 km² would continue to be retained as an Aboriginal Reserve.

Negotiations for the transfer were protracted. Alf Dyer, a lay missionary from Melbourne with experience at the Roper River Aboriginal Mission (founded in 1908), was approached and offered the position of Superintendent. Eventually he accepted and after many delays arrived at Oenpelli in September, 1925, (Cole 1972: 51).

While the newcomers made rapid in-roads into their country the Aborigines continued to follow aspects of their traditional life, collecting food in the billabongs and flats along the East Alligator River, performing some of the age-old rituals and painting the traditional designs in caves and on pieces of bark.

The Aborigines at Oenpelli today possess many stories about this contact period. They describe in great detail the feelings of the Aboriginal people on making acquaintance with 'white-fellows.' It was of interest to learn that on first acquaintance sugar was thought to be sand: the word in the local language for sugar is *kunkayalanj* which means sand.

Relations with the newcomers were not always harmonious and there is a series of small stones erected by Aborigines on the Red Lily Plains near Oenpelli which marks the site of a fatal clash between the two cultures.

It was not until the advent of aircraft, and later, four wheel drive vehicles, that the isolation of the Oenpelli community was broken and the Aborigines became fully exposed to the outside world with its pressures for development and progress.

CHAPTER 2

Rock Art Regions

The main physiographic unit of the Alligator Rivers Region is the Arnhem Land escarpment which is bounded by an often almost vertical west-facing scarp up to 300 metres high (Plate 4 top).

Associated with the escarpment are outlying sandstone massifs such as Mt Brockman-Nourlangie (Plate 4 bottom), Cannon Hill and Obiri Rock. These dominant topographic features are composed in the main of sandstones, conglomerates and quartzites of the Kombolgie formation.

A vast number of deep clefts and gorges have formed along margin joints and fault zones. The escarpment shows the result of erosion and consists largely of irregular forms with numerous caves and overhangs. Weathering of the outlying massifs is even more pronounced and some are honeycombed with caves and shelters (Plate 19 bottom). Indeed the whole landscape has been sculptured by relentless weathering to create an almost endless variety of scenic forms.

Typically, the less resistant rocks underlaying the sandstone erode more rapidly, undercutting the sandstone formation, which then collapses along minor vertical joint planes. Cliff-faces and waterfalls are therefore characteristic of this environment. Springs are also common, particularly at the foot of some of the major scarps, where they intersect water-bearing joints within the sandstone.

Erosion is still active throughout the area, especially at the major scarps, as shown by large fallen blocks which have accumulated at their base. Many of these have weathered to form rock shelters and overhangs used for many thousands of years by Aborigines for habitation and adopted in some instances as sacred sites of special significance.

35

The natural boundaries of the Alligator Rivers Region are related to the watersheds of the South and East Alligator Rivers (see Map 1). These rivers, in common with many other northern streams, rise on the plateau, cut a course along fault lines, descend the escarpment, often in picturesque waterfalls and associated gorges, and wind their way across the vast sub-coastal plains (Plate 19 top) towards Van Diemen Gulf.

The East Alligator River emerges from the plateau on to the plain upstream from Cahill's Crossing. It then meanders across the extensive, uniform and flat black soil plains. It is fed by Tin Camp and Magela Creeks. Cooper Creek drains the northern part of the region and joins the East Alligator in its main coastal inlet. The South Alligator River is joined by Nourlangie and Jim Jim Creeks; it too meanders across low-lying estuarine plains.

At the inland margins of the plains, the northward flowing rivers discharge into a disconnected series of long billabongs or wide, shallow swamps, flanked or choked by dense forests of *Melaleuca*. All the main rivers re-form seawards of this zone and rapidly widen into meandering estuarine channels, fringed with mangroves, which carry influxes of sea water in the dry season. A mosaic pattern of low-lying swampy ground with many channels and billabongs, fringes, and is often connected to, the main river channels.

The rivers are tidal; the salt water reaching upwards of fifty kilometres inland to provide an abundant supply of fish and crocodiles. Under this estuarine environment and seasonal flooding which cover the plains during the wet season, dense heavy clays have been formed with a common property of shrinkage and cracking (Hooper 1969: 111).

Aboriginal Occupation

The rivers of the region were arteries of life for Aborigines. They provided an abundant supply of food and served as a means of communication to the plateau. Combined with this the food resources of the vast wetlands (Plate 5 top) including those of Woolwonga and Magela, provide an ideal habitat for water-fowl of many species which frequent the area in tens of thousands. The rich food supplies of the river and flats are supplemented by game in the rocky hills, escarpment area and on the plateau, making the region one of the most suitable natural environments for man in Australia.

Evidence of long past occupation of the Alligator Rivers Region has been documented by White (1967: 149-151) who carried out an intensive archaeological survey of the area during 1964-1965. Evidence of continuous occupation over a long period came with the discovery of edge-ground axeheads during excavation of occupation deposits at one rock shelter. The finds have been dated to about 20 000 to 15 000 years ago. These are the earliest examples of edge-ground tools in the world (White 1967: 152).

A survey of sites, and excavation of five rock shelter deposits, provided a broadly consistent and coherent picture of the prehistory of the region. Generally speaking, two successive industrial traditions were distinguished. The earlier one occurs on the plain and in the valleys of the plateau and lasted from about 20 000 years to 6 500 years ago. The later industry occurs in two marked regions from about 6 500 years ago to the present.

Past Environmental Conditions

The Aboriginal world has not remained static since man first arrived in Australia. Mulvaney (1969: 57-58) describes how, during the last glaciation, sea-level dropped over one hundred metres below its present level, even 15 000 years ago it was perhaps seventy-five metres lower, only attaining its modern level between 6 000 and 3 600 years ago. On these figures, says Mulvaney, Australia has been severed from New Guinea for less than 8 000 years.

Changes in sea level had implications for the Alligator Rivers Region where the most striking difference in the environment 20 000 years ago was probably the absence of estuarine conditions as the sea was some 160 kilometres to the north.

White, (1971: 149) states that during the peak of the last glaciation the climate and economy of the plain near Oenpelli were much the same as those existing today in the broad, well-drained, plateau valleys. This theory would serve to explain why archaeological deposits in rock shelters on the plain, dated to 18 000 to 20 000 years ago, are so similar to those found in shelters in the plateau valley, dated as recently as the ethnographic present. All contain stone artifacts and occasional pieces of charcoal in coarse weathered sand, with scarcely a trace of bone or shell. This does not mean that food debris was always absent, but rather that it was destroyed more rapidly because the preservation agent, believed by White to be estuarine shell, was not present.

The evidence of the earliest landfall on the Australian-New Guinea landmass was drowned by the rising post-glacial sea. The 20 000 year old occupational debris in Arnhem Land was deposited by people who had already penetrated a great distance into their new homeland.

The climate of the area is monsoonal and markedly seasonal, with most rain falling between October and April. The annual average is about 1 400 millimetres (55 in.).

Seasonal changes had, and still do have, a profound effect on the behaviour of men and animals living in the region and the seasonal abundance of water in Arnhem Land is as much an ecological determining factor as is the scarcity of water in the central desert of Australia. During the wet season the plains become saturated and swamps overflow. Men and animals retreat to higher ground where they congregate in the same way as fauna clusters around permanent water-holes in arid regions. During the wet, the Aborigines could not reach the swamp plants or estuarine fauna; but as the rains slackened and the dry season advanced, movement became easier and they could range over a wider area in their quest for food.

The ready availability of dry rock shelters in the outliers, along the river gorges and at the base of the escarpment, provided comfortable occupation shelters for the Aborigines.

As Spencer (1928: 823) noted: 'The shelters were overhung with shelving rocks all round the top of the hill, so that they could change their camps to suit the changing weather. If the wind and rain blew in from the north, all they had to do was pick up their few belongings and take their fire-sticks round to the shelters on the south side. The shelters were indeed such that they could accommodate themselves to any kind of weather.'

It is in these shelters that the Aborigines clustered during the wet season and it is on these walls and ceilings that they painted an extensive range of colourful ochre designs of importance to their sacred beliefs and for a range of other purposes.

Early References to Art

Cahill, who had made seasonal visits to the Alligator Rivers Region from the 1880s, was probably the first non-Aboriginal to investigate in some detail the rock shelters of the Region. His close association with the *Kakadu* group gave him an understanding of the life of these people.

Another recorded description of the art was provided by H. Stockdale, a pioneer squatter on the Adelaide River, who explored the country on and adjacent to the Alligator Rivers in 1891. Stockdale (S.A.A. 1891: 790-791) in a letter to T. Worsnop, Town Clerk of Adelaide, described the discovery of some forty caves within a distance travelled of 160 kilometres, in which there were numerous cave paintings, '. . . hieroglyphics and skeletons laid out in regular lines. Some of the drawings and hieroglyphics are very remarkable indeed and some cases it is the roof, in others the sides, of the caves that are painted upon; these drawings consist of animals, birds, reptiles, men, women, canoes, canoes with men in them, and a great many of the drawings of the men show mouths; the hieroglyphics resemble in some measure Greek letters; one very remarkable drawing of a man with his arms crossed over his breast and two peculiar little tufts . . . [protruding] from the crown of his head, a necklace around the neck; the breast covered with a regular device in straight lines, the stomach with lines at regular intervals . . . the wall was adorned with a spiral and a number of hieroglyphics was found in the same vault or cave that contained the skeleton, the face of the man was really well drawn; I should think altogether there would be quite 200 different drawings though sometimes one cave would have quite seven or eight different representations more or less mixed together.'

Stockdale applied to the South Australian Department of Education for a grant to photograph and record this series of sites; unfortunately, the request was refused.

Attempts to find further details of the original finds has failed except for the location in the Mitchell Library, Sydney, of a series of small, rather poor sketches by Stockdale of Aborigines, flora and fauna labelled 'East Alligator River'.

In October 1893 the Government Resident of the Northern Territory, C. J. Dashwood, visited the Alligator Rivers Region. The party arrived early in October by steam launch at Alowangeewan, a temporary camp formed by Messrs Cahill and Johnston, who had for some months been buffalo shooting in this locality. Alowangeewan was situated on the north side of the East Alligator river, about twenty kilometres upstream. Dashwood provides an account of his investigations, '. . . with the assistance of Mr Cahill's boat, the *Polly*, we arrived at Unmooragee which is a small belt of jungle situated about two miles [3.2 km] south of the river, on the edge of a grassed plain. I decided to leave some of the horses and stores here and take a lighter kit, sufficient for a few days, and examine the country on either side of the East Alligator. This was done accordingly. For a distance of about forty-five miles [72 km] from the mouth the country generally consists of open grassed plains, dark loam, with clay and clay subsoil, subject to inundation in the wet season; the grasses very succulent on the plains. The long coarse grass seems to have been replaced by the shorter, nutritious ones, due no doubt to the herds of buffalo which have been depasturing on these plains for many years. Intervening belts of forest country were crossed. Here the soil is a loose, friable, sandy loam; poorer grasses, stringybark, and woollybutt, stunted cabbage, and fan palms plentiful; belts of large paperbarks skirt the numerous swamps. The rough broken tableland country commences at about forty-five miles [72.4 km]

39

from the mouth. Here some fine billabongs of fresh water were met with, amongst others Annerwerleke, Owenpelly (Umberlamyon), Oo-ay were the principal ones. These waters are in my opinion permanent; each is about half mile [.8 km] in length, abounding in waterfowl and fish, and covered with lilies. In this vicinity the sandstone hills are rough and precipitous, rising almost perpendicularly for some 400 ft [121.9 m] or 500 ft [152.4 m], with detached masses of rock at the base. Under an immense slab of sandstone, which was resting on other slabs, affording good shelter for man and beast, an aboriginal gallery of pictures was seen — alligators, kangaroo, fish, wallabies, birds, and human figures were drawn with coloured chalks. This is approximately the position where, in June, 1866, Mr John McKinlay and party camped for three weeks on account of heavy rains, the ground being too soft to travel. The natives attacked his party, but were driven off. The tribe are still hostile, keeping to the ranges, and showing no disposition to exchange compliments with the whites.

'Whilst on the eastern side of the river a herd of about sixty buffaloes were seen, and through the skill of Mr Cahill some excellent beef was secured, equal to the best English cattle. About 1 200 head of buffalo have been shot in the locality during the past few months, merely for the sake of the horns and hides.

'I am considerably impressed with the extent and fertility of the lands contiguous to this river.'

The party later returned to Unmooragee. 'This is a favorite camping ground for the natives', states Dashwood, 'I was surprised and alarmed to find several undoubtedly suffering from leprosy. In one case the fingers of both hands were gone, merely the stumps remaining; in another the toes had all decayed away, and others disfigured about the face. They evidently understood the loathsomeness of the disease, and were afraid, for very soon they disappeared. I am informed by Mr Cahill that he has seen, during the few months he has been in the district, over fifty natives affected in the same way.' (Rep. of N.T. 1897: 8).

Dashwood was later to report on the increased strain in relations between Europeans and Aborigines on the north coast. (Rep. of N.T. 1899).

Pioneer Anthropological Studies

It was the great Australian ethnographer, Sir Baldwin Spencer, who was the first anthropologist to observe the sites and document the life and culture of the *Kakadu* people of the Alligator Rivers Region.

40

In 1910 the Government appointed Spencer as a member of a Preliminary Scientific Expedition to investigate different phases of the Aboriginal 'question'. In this capacity he visited the Northern Territory and, in June, 1912, went to Paddy Cahill's settlement at Oenpelli to study the customs of the people.

Spencer (1928: 823-824) describes his visit to the cave at the top of the hill (Inyalak) about one kilometre from Oenpelli: 'The most interesting things, and what we came up to see, were the rock shelters of the natives, where they rest in the cool of the evening during fine weather, or are protected from the monsoonal rains during the wet season, when the flats below are transformed into swamps.

'The slanting roofs and sides were one mass of native drawings, precisely similar to those done on bark, but here, the rocks had been blackened for long years by the smoke of countless camp fires and the drawings, most of them fishes, had been superimposed on one another, the brighter colours of the more recent ones standing out clearly on the darker background. Here and there were groups of stencilled hands and feet. On other rock shelters on the hills along the Alligator River, the drawings were not superimposed and comprised fishes, turtles, crocodiles and snakes. Very rarely there was a drawing such as the one which represented a gnome-like creature.'

In Spencer's opinion (1914: 439) the bark and rock paintings of the area represented the highest artistic level amongst Australian Aborigines, 'with the possible exception of the Melville and Bathurst Islanders, whose art, however, shows indications of the influence of some culture outside that of the Australian Continent.'

Three years later Dyer, who took charge of the mission in 1925, visited Oenpelli to deliver stores to Cahill. He describes how he '. . . first saw the native ochre drawings on the Oenpelli Hill, as it was then called, when Paddy Cahill was there. Oenpelli . . . Inyalak is the native name . . . Even at that time it was considered a show place for visitors.'

Dyer (1934, chap. 6: 1) went on '. . . it is a lovely view to see from the rock [Inyalak] in the distance an outcrop from among the trees about thirty miles [48.2 km] away where the kangaroo jumped when he came across from Asia . . . All their stories link them with the East and the Rainbow story seems to be told in different ways in each tribe, yet mixed up with the birth of children.

'Upon the first visit, there was a platform for a dead person where the chief mourners had to sit under the droppings . . . other caves had bones and skulls piled on top of one another . . . I copied a drawing of a devil. It was high up and the weather had washed it away. It is a combination of animals, the foundation stone of most of their beliefs, with a strong element of evil spirits, of which they are so afraid.'

Ten years later when in residence, he suggested to C. P. Mountford '. . . that if some of the top ones could be removed carefully, those underneath might be very interesting, for they are painted on top of others . . . In one cave near Oenpelli I once saw the drawing of an X-ray woman; drawn with all the internal organs. Major, who was the best native artist I knew, did many drawings on bark for me. The kangaroo painted by Major is one of the best I have seen.'

Dyer describes how '. . . the natives in the Blue Mud Bay area painted a lot on their bark huts. Some were quite interesting and the hills behind may have some art treasures. Around Roper River their drawings are more primitive. One large cave is full of human bones, which must have a gruesome story behind it. It is full of human hand drawings, so common throughout Australia. As the hand was held on the wall, it was painted with white pipe clay between the fingers. Many of the drawings at Oenpelli are on the roofs where it must have been difficult to paint. The work is done with a brush made out of bark or fibrous wood.

'These X-ray drawings are very interesting, especially the woman showing correctly the position of the organs. I never thought of teaching them to draw or paint. Some of them watch me sometimes, but express no desire to try. The children in school, when left to themselves, followed their native way of art.'

The first published account of the Oenpelli sites was prepared by Tindale (1928: 35-37). He describes the sites in some detail: 'On the sides of a sandstone hill overlooking the East Alligator River, about a mile [1.6 km] to the eastward from the former Government Experimental Station (now converted into an Aborigines' reserve) there are several caves and rock-shelters used by the natives of the *Kakadu* tribe as occasional dwellings and as repositories for the bones of their dead.

'The first of these shelters to be noticed has been weathered out of the horizontally bedded stone and forms a chamber six feet [1.8 m] long with an overhang of some eight feet [2.4 m] and the maximum height of four feet [1.2 m].

'As far back as the present generation of natives can remember, it has been used as a wet season camping place. The floor is built up of layers of ashes and debris, resulting from their occupation. Every portion of the roof is covered with paintings. Red, white and yellow are used, one layer superimposed upon several earlier layers in such a way that the final effects are very complex . . . Most figures are representations of barramundi but turtles, mammals, and other creatures are depicted occasionally.'

Superimpositions on earlier representations were noted. Tindale also describes X-ray art: 'The internal anatomy of many of the creatures is figured in detail, the back-bone is usually conspicuous and prominence is given also to the liver and fat-bodies. Since the natives of all the tribes of Arnhem Land suffer from chronic "fat-hunger", such sources of supply are of great importance to them.' Tindale noticed that the figures in the galleries were painted in a similar technique to those executed by *Kakadu* men on sheets of bark and illustrated by Spencer.

'In a second shelter near the first there are many paintings of anthropomorphic forms . . . On the same hill, there is a third shelter beneath a projecting sandstone block. The low entrance is marked by a branched stick five feet [1.5 m] high, which is supported by a mound of pebbles. It has unascertained ceremonial significance [probably a marker to denote a burial place].

'The walls and roof are covered with figures of hands, each one outlined in white pipe-clay. Scattered about the floor are the remains of many human beings. Among them several dozen complete skulls and fragments of many others were noticed. Some of the bones still remained in the stringy-bark parcels and string-and-grass dilly bags in which they had been carried to the shelter. Most of the containers, however, were old and perishing. Some were of large size (up to two feet [60.9 cm] in length and a foot [30.4 cm] in width). Not all contained human remains; one, for example, contained only a single ball of native beeswax (about two inches [5 cm] in diameter).'

Tindale describes how the *Kakadu* people wrapped the body of deceased persons in stringy or paper-bark and placed it in the fork of a tree. After the flesh had decayed and the concluding ceremonies incidental to the mourning period had been performed, the bones were gathered in a painted bark-bag or other receptacle and deposited in one of several shelters and caves. No trouble was taken to preserve the identity of the remains after they had been placed in the caves amongst the bones of former tribesmen.

The American-Australian Scientific Expedition to Arnhem Land

Detailed study and recording of the large and impressive body of art in the Alligator Rivers Region did not begin until 1948 when the American-Australian Scientific Expedition to Arnhem Land visited Oenpelli between September and November, 1948.

This important expedition was initiated in 1945 when Mountford was on a successful lecture tour of the United States. While in

America he applied to the National Geographic Society for a grant to make an expedition to Arnhem Land and adjacent regions to undertake ethnological and photographic recording among the Aborigines. This application was accepted and planning began in 1946 for an expedition to enter Arnhem Land early in the following year.

Full co-operation came from many quarters. The National Geographic Society and the Smithsonian Institution of Washington, offered to make members of their staffs available; the Commonwealth Minister for Information undertook to meet travel and transport costs; the Minister for Air offered air transport, wherever possible; the Minister for the Army allowed the expedition to draw on Army stores for food and equipment; the Minister for Health arranged for a unit of three scientists from the Institute of Anatomy to join the expedition, their object being to study Aboriginal health and nutrition; the Minister for the Interior placed his Northern Territory organisation at the disposal of Mountford and offered assistance with transport arrangements and the forwarding of mails and supplies; the Council for Scientific and Industrial Research released a navigator and engineer to run a trawler for the party. With so much co-operation and help, considerable progress had been made by the end of 1946.

However, delays occurred and it was not until the beginning of 1948 that the final party had been selected and arrangements made for transport and supplies. The party left for Darwin in March, 1948, and was in Arnhem Land until November.

The expedition established four research camps while in the field: Groote Eylandt, Roper River, Yirrkala and Oenpelli. Each camp was situated in different environmental situations.

In selecting Oenpelli, Mountford had estimated that it would be the most spectacular and most productive area for study. He states in the official records of the expedition (V. 1, 1956: xxviii): 'Looking from our tent doors, we could see a placid lagoon, dotted with water-lilies and numberless birds and fringed with green rushes; on the distant shore was the eucalyptus forest; beyond that the brown buffalo-grass flood plain, and behind that, again, the high escarpment of the rugged Arnhem Land plateau, blue with the haze of distance.

'Oenpelli offered a varied field for all; the naturalists, the anthropologists and the photographers. It has three distinct physical environments, each rich in its own flora and fauna; the open savannah woodlands, the black soil flood plains of the Alligator Rivers, and the forbidding plateau country in the caves of which we were to find relics of early man and innumerable aboriginal paintings.'

Mountford's study of the art of Oenpelli and other regions was the most comprehensive to have been undertaken. He found two of the mediums through which Aboriginal artists expressed themselves; on cave walls and on sheets of bark.

Mountford (1956: 109) considers the cave paintings of the Oenpelli area to be more skilfully executed and more varied in design than in any other part of Arnhem Land: '. . . in fact, they are the most numerous and beautiful series of cave paintings that we know of in Australia. The bark paintings of Oenpelli, on the other hand, do not differ greatly from the basic art of Arnhem Land, i.e. single or multiple figures in a plain ground, except that they have been modified on one hand by the X-ray art, and on the other by the art of the caves.'

During the seven weeks the expedition was camped at Oenpelli, Mountford found an extensive series of cave paintings at Inyalak Hill (Plate 8), and at Inagurdurwil, near Red Lily Lagoon and in adjacent areas. In addition to these cave painting localities he learnt from the Aborigines of other sites at Tor Rock, Cooper Creek, and in caves south of Obiri. 'There is little doubt', says Mountford, 'that many more galleries could be found in both the western face of the Arnhem Land Plateau and its residuals on the Alligator flood plains. A rich field probably awaits the investigator who is prepared to spend time and energy searching for further galleries of cave paintings in those places.'

This statement proved to be prophetic as Brandl, Chaloupka, Edwards and others, have discovered large numbers of sites in these regions and made records of many of the designs. During the recent survey, some three hundred sites were examined and found to contain vast numbers of paintings in every known Arnhem Land style (see Map 2).

Main Oenpelli Art Styles

Mountford (1956: 112) examined carefully the Oenpelli cave painting sites and divided the motifs into two widely differing styles. They are polychrome (many colours) X-ray paintings of animals, birds, reptiles and fish (but seldom of human beings) in which both the external and internal details are indicated, many having been painted within the memory of living man; and single-line monochrome (one colour) drawings which, the Aborigines claim, are not painted by men but by spirit people called *Mimi*.

Polychrome X-ray Art: Although Aboriginal art is fundamentally visual, X-ray art is, in addition, intellectual. The Aboriginal artists of Oenpelli not only paint what they see, but also what they know

Flooded black
soil plains

East Alligator
River crossing

Arnhem Land
escarpment

Obiri Rocks

Stone arrangements

Jabiluka

Abraded grooves

TIDAL ARM OF EAST ALLIGATOR

MAIN ROCK SHELTER

to be present but cannot see; the skeleton, heart, lungs, stomach, intestines and other organs of the body.

Although this remarkable art was used in simple form in several parts of the world, it reached its highest development in western Arnhem Land. The range of subjects in X-ray style, and the manner of depicting them is somewhat limited; birds, fish and animals, but seldom man. The subjects of the X-ray artists seldom show any movement although those which figure on some bark paintings are quite animated. It is essentially a static art. X-ray art has a general distribution throughout the Alligator Rivers Region and examples were found at most of the sites investigated.

Monochrome Mimi Art: The *'Mimi'* artists, whoever they might have been, had a strong feeling for composition and movement. Their main subject was man in action; running, fighting and throwing spears. *Mimi* paintings were executed in red, which, according to local myth, was made up of blood and red ochre. It is possible that the *Mimi* art of Oenpelli developed from the simple 'stick' figures so common in Australian cave art. For instance, there are numerous galleries in the Cobar district of western New South Wales which feature small human 'stick' figures in a range of hunting activities.

A remarkable feature of the *Mimi* style is its likeness to similar figures in Europe and Africa. Although there has been extensive over-painting of X-ray paintings, this characteristic was not often seen in the *Mimi* drawings. Groups of *Mimi* drawings, some comprising as many as thirty figures, appear to have been complete compositions in themselves, conceived and carried out by one artist at one time.

Mimi art provides important evidence of the past life and culture of the Aborigines of the region. Hunting scenes are quite common. Weapons and other artifacts are shown in great detail and even mortuary rites are depicted. Battle scenes, involving large groups of figures, feature at some sites.

47

The Main Oenpelli Sites

Thirty-two sites of cave paintings were located and investigated in the area between Oenpelli and the East Alligator River (see Map 2).

The main art sites at Oenpelli are located on Inyalak Hill (Plate 8) which is a residual of the Arnhem Land plateau. It is about two kilometres long, one kilometre wide and approximately 180 metres in height. The summit is heavily eroded into a maze of steep-sided vertical chasms, huge tumbled boulders and extensive rock shelters in which Aborigines have made seasonal camps for many centuries. In some shelters, the ceilings and walls are covered with mosaics of cave paintings; in other places there are only a few scattered designs.

The main Inyalak shelter is an outstanding example of an Aboriginal painted gallery with dozens of brightly coloured figures covering almost every available surface (Plate 7 bottom). Fish are the main subject with turtles, kangaroos and most other food animals represented.

These sites range in extent from small overhangs to large shelters with associated cave-like passages. Many sites were used to lodge human remains at the termination of mortuary ceremonies and in a number of shelters red ochred human bones were found. In most instances, the remains have been disturbed and strewn over the cave floors.

Painting styles at most sites include *Mimi* figures depicted in a range of hunting scenes and other outstanding, large stylized spirit figures, polychrome X-ray paintings of fish, tortoises, kangaroos and other food animals, were superimposed upon older style paintings. Hand stencils and impressions were noted at some sites.

There were also many culture contact paintings, in particular ships identified as of Macassan, Dutch and British origin. These paintings are accurate representations of vessels that sailed up the nearby East Alligator River to deliver stores to Cahill's Landing *en route* for Oenpelli (Plate 12 top left). The coastal people also were known to visit the inland groups and no doubt carried with them accounts of the new arrivals seen on the coast.

The condition of the paintings is generally disappointing. Weathering, intense water wash, moulds, insect and animal damage, have taken a toll and many sites contain only weathered remnants of paintings. Others contain a few well preserved figures of importance to comparative studies of art styles.

Evidence of intensive occupation is obvious in most shelters; the floors are scattered with bones, shells, ashes and other debris. Most sites are on the edge of the black soil plains and many near large lagoons, including the well known Red Lily Lagoon.

Cave Paintings at Inagurdurwil

One of the main sites is known as *Inagurdurwil*. It is situated on a spur of the Arnhem Land Plateau which extends on to the flood plains of the East Alligator River. Most of the paintings are on vertical rock-faces or in shallow caves. The terrain is particularly rugged and so the paintings tend to be grouped in the most suitable situations.

There are some important paintings at this site. Figures of two males complete with hunting spears and smaller goose spears (recorded by Leichhardt in 1845), goose wing fans, and wearing head and elbow ornaments. *Mimi* figures are numerous; one scene showing a ceremony being performed with nine dancing figures and another playing the didjeridu. Hunting and fighting scenes are a feature and also a number of spirit figures in several colours.

Outstanding among the contact paintings is that of a steamer complete with funnels, ventilators, masts, derricks and the fore and aft hatch covers. This particular site is the best of the series in this area. Unfortunately, their general condition is poor and few will survive unless protective measures are taken.

In general, these sites do not compare favourably with the rich array of paintings at Inyalak Hill and others to the north and east of Oenpelli.

During the Alligator Rivers Region Environmental Fact Finding Study a large number of photographic records was made to add to Mountford's excellent record (1956: 109-264). There is an urgent need to undertake detailed comparative studies before the remaining paintings deteriorate further.

Art of Cooper and Tin Camp Creek Region

To the east of Oenpelli lies the watershed of Cooper and Tin Camp Creeks. Several exploratory trips were made into the general area of Cooper and Tin Camp Creeks (Plate 40 top) in the northern sector of the Alligator Rivers Region in the Arnhem Land Aboriginal Reserve. These were undertaken to gain an overall record of rock art in this region for the purpose of comparison with sites to the south.

As a result, it was possible to obtain some information about sites from Aboriginal owners who normally reside at Oenpelli.

Some seventy sites were located in the headwaters of the two major rivers (see Map 2) and no doubt many other occurrences will be found as this vast and rugged area is surveyed.

Cooper and Tin Camp Creeks rise on opposite sides of a rugged divide. Cooper Creek flows north and then north-east on to the Murgenella Plains near Mt Borrodaile, while Tin Camp Creek flows west into the East Alligator River above the first gorge.

Mt Borrodaile (see Map 1) is itself an art and burial site. The mountain has been almost hollowed out by weathering to form large overhangs and a network of tunnels and cavities.

Polychrome female paintings of a distinctive style predominate in the art. There are many other styles including contact paintings, mainly of different types of boats.

There are several hundred dilly bags containing human bones deposited in the different caves and shelters. Skeletons have been placed also on many rock ledges.

The mountain and associated residuals are sited adjacent to the Murgenella Plains where plentiful supplies of food are readily available.

Mt Borrodaile has been visited by Macintosh and Evans who describe it (pers. comm.) as outstanding, both in the range and quality of the art and in the fact that it has not been disturbed.

A well known site of importance in this general area is Nimbuwah, a striking residual set in the alluvial plain some thirty-two kilometres to the north-east of Oenpelli (Plate 9). This dominant feature has legendary significance for the Aborigines who associate it with a mythological hero, *Nimbuwah*. At its base is a series of weathered cave paintings. The area (N.T. Portion 1301) is prescribed in an attempt to ensure its protection. The photograph of Nimbuwah has been included in this report with the express approval of the Aboriginal owners of the site.

Three Aborigines guided me to sites in the region of Cooper Creek and Nimbuwah. Two were from the *Mirarr* group: Mary Gurindjulu Ganaraj (*Ngalngarridj* sub-section; *Yarri-burrik* semi-moiety; *Ngalngarradjku* and *Dua* moieties), Marjorie Cooper (*Ngalbulanj* sub-section, *Yarri-burrik* semi-moiety; *Ngalngarradjku* and *Dua* moieties) and one was from the *Madjawarr* group: Joseph Gamaraidj Giradbul (*Nabulanj* sub-section; *Yarri-burrik* semi-moiety; *Nangarradjku* and *Dua* moieties). Peter Carroll, a linguist resident at Oenpelli, joined the party to assist in a site survey of the area.

Sacred Site Surveys

A number of sites of sacred significance has been identified during surveys undertaken by Carroll (1973: 1-23). At the insistence of Aboriginal owners, six sites were surveyed by Lands Branch surveyors in August, 1972, with the object of initiating procedures to bring them under the *Native and Historical Objects and Areas Preservation Ordinance, 1955-1961*. The sites concerned were as follows:

- *The Green Ant Site—"Gabo"*, is a group of low hills south-west of Nabarlek. A series of boulders in close proximity to the Queensland Mines base camp are the 'eggs' of the site and are an important part of it.

- *The Star Site—"Mankinkinhkani"* or *"Mankokkarrng"*, is approximately five kilometres west of Nabarlek. It consists of escarpment face, including a number of peaks, and the surrounding area. The access road to Nabarlek passes within approximately one kilometre of the site (N.T. Portion 1442).

- *The Brown Snake Site—"Yirrbardbard"* or *"Dadbe"*, is approximately eight kilometres N.N.E. of Nabarlek and consists of escarpment face and surrounding area (N.T. Portion 1396).

- *Lightning Site—"Namarrkon"*, is approximately sixteen kilometres east of Nabarlek. It consists of escarpment face with a creek and surrounding area including a number of small hills (N.T. Portion 1444).

- *The Children's Site—"Njibinjibinj"*, approximately ten kilometres east of Nabarlek and consists of a series of sandstone outcrops arranged in the shape of a semi-circle and the area within the semi-circle (N.T. Portion 1443).

- *Myra Falls—"Kudjumarndi"*, approximately sixteen kilometres south of Nabarlek and consists of the falls and surrounding country, including areas upstream and downstream along the Tin Camp

Creek. The big pool below the falls is in the centre and the most important part of the site (N.T. Portion 1393).

Several of these sites were visited with the Aboriginal owners who evinced great satisfaction at the steps being taken to reserve features of legendary and sacred importance in their culture.

The Aborigines who guided the party through the area stopped twenty-seven kilometres north-east of Oenpelli and visited an important cave called *Djimuban*. This rock shelter is part of the 'Old Women Site', *(Kabulurr)*, and is situated about sixteen kilometres north-west of Nabarlek near Birraduk Creek, the main tributary of Cooper Creek. It consists of a sandstone outcrop and surrounding area separated from the main escarpment.

There is an inseparable association between mythology and painted galleries. The legend associated with this particular area concerns an old woman who came from the west, travelling along the East Alligator River and up the landing creek to Oenpelli, where she left her dog. She kept going and settled at a place near Birraduk Creek where she made camp and went swimming in a nearby water-hole. The river came up and she was drowned and became a rock where she is now. Aborigines are forbidden to climb over this rock.

A prominent feature of the escarpment situated about two kilometres from the painted gallery is also of legendary significance and concerns a mythological hero named *Kunmayimbuk*. He came from the west travelling along Cooper Creek. Another man, *Yirriyu*, came from the north and met *Kunmayimbuk*. They had a long fight about fire as *Yirriyu* had none and *Kunmayimbuk* had some. They separated and *Yirriyu* went north to his place and *Kunmayimbuk* went to Birraduk Creek where he is now. During the wet season the water is always clear near *Kunmayimbuk* because he had fire but near *Yirriyu* it is dark because he had no fire.

The rock painting site is of special importance to Joseph Giradbul and his brother, Frank Nalowed (*Nabulanj* sub-section; *Yarri-burrik* semi-moiety; *Nangarrandjku* and *Dua* moieties). Their father (*Madjumbu*) painted in the shelter some sixty years ago when it was used as a wet weather camp for his family. Evidence of occupation is present on the shelter floor in the form of bones, ash and other debris.

Joseph claimed that the figures were painted on the walls before his father went hunting to give some 'help' in the chase. Sometimes figures were commenced before leaving to hunt and would be completed upon return.

Several hundred polychrome figures decorate the main back wall of the shelter. Generally, they are well protected and there is no sign of deterioration of the main figures. As in many instances, designs on the more exposed parts of the cave walls have suffered damage. Superimposition, characteristic of wet weather occupation shelters, is a feature of this gallery.

The main central figure is of a crocodile in X-ray style and nearby there is a kangaroo (Plate 10 middle left and right). Barramundi, catfish and other species, also figure in the gallery. There are colourful spirit figures, and hand stencils.

The site is one of the best examples of X-ray art in the Alligator Rivers Region and its comparatively small size and natural shape, lends it to protection from weathering by some form of enclosure.

The valley of Tin Camp Creek is wide and fertile. In its uppermost reaches are the sacred Myra Falls *(Kudjumarndi)*. This area was an excellent environment with plentiful food resources. In past times, different groups met there for ceremonies. Local legend tells how there was an orphan camped in the area with a group of people. He cried for his mother. His relatives offered him different types of food but he kept on crying for his mother. They told him to stop crying or the Rainbow Serpent would come and get him. He kept crying and the Rainbow Serpent came and devoured all those people (Carroll 1973: 14).

Rock shelters along both sides of the valley contain paintings. There is a wide range of art at these sites, including every known Arnhem Land style.

European contact paintings increase towards the coast and many fine examples occur in rock shelters in this region. At one major site there is an interesting buffalo hunt superimposed over a large painting of a salt water crocodile (Plate 39 top).

One of the major sites examined near the divide of Cooper and Tin Camp Creeks is known by the name of *Djarrng*. This site does not have strong taboos associated with it and was a wet weather shelter rather than a sacred site. There is a series of cliff overhangs

56

along the side of the rugged escarpment. This has been a favourite campsite and was visited by the mythological hero, *Mankung*, while he was looking for wild honey. He searched in vain so he went east and found some honey in an area called *Makani*. He put the honey in his dillybag and returned to another site called *Kudjumarndi*. As he approached the camp he heard loud underground noises. He dropped everything and ran away to hide. He crept back and saw a big flood so he collected his things and returned to where he found the honey. He stayed there and that place is now *Mankung Djang*. There was lots of wild honey there but now there are only stinging insects.

The gallery of art at this site is extensive, covering the base of the cliffs for several hundred metres. There are three life-size buffaloes with X-ray and other polychrome art styles superimposed over them. As buffalo probably reached this area in the 1840s, this dates the recent art to the last 130 years.

An interesting group of human figures depicts a burial ceremony being performed. The body of the deceased is lying on a special platform (Plate 17 top). X-ray style paintings, *Mimi* figures, spirit beings and a range of food animals combine to form an impressive gallery of Aboriginal art.

Beeswax Figures

Two well preserved small human figures formed on the rock surface in beeswax were found at this site (Plate 11). Such designs are generally rare but do occur in small numbers at most sites in the Alligator Rivers Region. Evans (1964: 18) first recorded the use of wax pellets in association with rock paintings. He found several examples at a small site near the waterhole known as *Gumaduk* during an expedition to open a road between Oenpelli and Maningrida. A number of human figures formed of beeswax and rows of wax pellets pressed on the rock surface was found in 1965 by Brandl (1968: 19-29) at sites in the region of Cahill's Crossing, the upper East Alligator River and near Magela Creek. Chaloupka has also located a number of excellent examples at remoter sites.

58

Engraved grooves — East Alligator River — Cannon Hill — Oenpelli track — Inagurdurwil Hill — Red Lily Lagoon

The Aborigines of north-eastern Arnhem Land are expert at modelling small animal and human figures, called *Kamou korngi*, from the wax of wild bees. This wax, much more plastic than that of the European bee, when warmed slightly is moulded into shape with the fingers. When the craftsman is satisfied with his modelling, he paints the figures with designs. These sometimes indicate the moiety and *mata* (language group) of the totemic creature. McCarthy (1962: 57) figures a kangaroo, a turtle and a crocodile from a Yirrkala collection presented to The Australian Museum by Rev. F. W. Chaseling.

Other examples of beeswax figures were collected at Yirrkala by Mountford (1956: 445) and in north-east Arnhem Land by Berndt and Berndt (1964: 374-375). Among these figures was one of the boomerang-man *Oijal*, and one of his wives, *Neri-neri*. McConnel (1953: 19, 35) records a waxen human figure used in increase ceremonies in Cape York and Elkin and the Berndts claim that several Yirrkala figures were used in imitative love 'magic' and to cause the death of an enemy.

The condition of the figures and designs found in rock shelter galleries differs considerably; some are badly cracked and the wax faded while others are in sound condition. No great antiquity is possible for these figures as they are composed of perishable organic substance exposed to the elements. In view of the comparatively small number of examples, some special significance for these unusual figures seems highly probable.

An impressive gallery of art in a high rock overhang was located in a secluded valley a few kilometres from *Djarrng*. Many paintings in white pigments overlie earlier weathered designs. Among these are two paintings of Chinese men riding on vehicles (Plate 12 bottom right). These were identified by an Aboriginal of the *Danek* group, David Namilmil Mangiru (*Nawamud* sub-section; *Yarri-yaning* semi-moiety; *Nangarradjku* and *Yirridja* moieties), as related to construction of the Pine Creek-Darwin railway in 1886-89. Other introduced animals and also guns are depicted in this art. The evidence of these sites supports the contention that Aborigines continued to live a

61

Plate 20 An interesting group of painted designs on an isolated outcrop at Cannon Hill. The painting of a spider is unusual. Most galleries in this area show evidence of general deterioration.

traditional way of life and painted in their galleries at least until recent times.

Sites have been reported also from the Wellington Range near the coast (see Map 1). A feature of the art in this region is the great number of culture contact paintings; praus, sailing ships, guns, revolvers, knives, buffaloes and other introduced stock. One of the main sites is at Black Rock, a residual outlier of the range; it takes its name from the dark patinated surface of granular sandstone of which it is composed. The site contains a large and important gallery of paintings. The central subject is a salt-water crocodile some four and a half metres long (Plate 39 bottom). Other paintings include a one and a half metre high lotus lily plant in polychrome and a Macassan dagger in its sheath, carefully painted in X-ray style with a red ochre outline and interior design, over an off-white background.

This site is of archaeological importance as there is a surface scatter of animal bones, shells and glass fragments, including a piece of Chinese porcelain. Several human skulls also are protruding through the deposits.

Smaller galleries are located around the base of the outlier. Subjects depicted in these shelters are in the main different types of seacraft of European origin, e.g. sailing boats and steamers.

Other paintings of contact subjects occur on a large group of rocks eroded into eighteen metre high blocks. An excellent representation of a Macassan prau is among the interesting paintings at this site (Chaloupka, pers. comm.).

Early contact with Macassan and European navigators was recorded by Aborigines in the rock shelters of the north coast, possibly in an attempt to allay the influence of the new arrivals. Turner (1973: 286-315) has provided an example of the range of this interesting art recorded during detailed studies on Bickerton Island, located off Groote Eylandt.

It is of interest that contact paintings throughout Australia are naturalistic, even in central Australia where Aborigines portrayed their totemic beings of the Dreamtime in simple line, circle, track and abstract style. Contact period paintings depict events and forms in naturalistic silhouettes. In the Alligator Rivers Region, such paintings are static. It may be inferred that the animated style of the *Mimi* painters was lost at some unknown time in the past.

The north coast area was beyond the present study but it contains many art sites of obvious importance.

It is relevant to any consideration of the preservation of representative examples of Arnhem Land art styles, that extensive and well-preserved sites exist within the area of the Arnhem Land Reserve. It might be expected that these sites will remain under Aboriginal custody. To date, the remoteness of the area, and the restricted access have served to a large degree to discourage visitors and at the request of the Aborigines concerned, no detailed data is given in respect of the precise locations of sites.

It may be concluded that the significance of the sites to living people appears to be greater in the northern sector of the Alligator Rivers Region than in the very southern section in the general region of Jim Jim Falls.

Obiri Rock

In the region of the East Alligator River Crossing there are many irregular sandstone residuals which rise abruptly out of extensive alluvial plains and low soil and laterite covered ridges. Differential erosion has given rise to numerous caves and overhangs; cross-bedding, ripple marks and occasional pebble beds can be seen in the sandstone sequence.

In common with the occupation shelters of the Oenpelli, Cooper Creek, Tin Camp Creek and Mt Borrodaile areas, the distribution of rock art sites is related to food supplies. As will be demonstrated in this report, art was an integral part of daily life. Regions which possessed the most prolific food resources were the places where Aborigines spent most of their time. It follows that their sacred art and that decorating the walls of wet weather occupation shelters are in close proximity to the rivers and associated lagoons and alluvial flats.

Unlike many parts of Australia, the availability of suitable rock shelters, overhangs and caves, was not a determining factor in the distribution of art sites. In the Alligator Rivers Region, there are great numbers of suitable shelters throughout the area, largely composed of sandstones of the Kombolgie formation. This situation is obvious at Obiri Rock (*Ubir*) where there are outstanding examples of Aboriginal rock art in large out-cropping residuals (Plate 43 top). Some thirty-six sites have been found in close proximity to the main Obiri gallery (Plate 13 bottom).

During Mountford's seven weeks at Oenpelli in 1948, he learnt of galleries at Obiri Rock and Cannon Hill. The following year he returned with a small party to photograph the paintings for inclusion in a book for UNESCO (Mountford 1954: 1).

Mountford (1956: 163), was impressed with the main gallery of paintings (Plate 14 top) situated under a deep overhang on the western side of a comparatively small isolated monolith. The back wall of this gallery is a smooth, curving, vertical face of rock, about fifteen

65

Plate 22 Examples of superimposed figures in one of the rock shelters at the base of Mt Brockman. The site is of great importance to Aborigines who believed one of their mythical culture heroes transformed the King Brown Snake into a rainbow which now lives in a rock-hole on the Mount.

metres long and two metres high and covered by a frieze of X-ray paintings. The designs are mainly large representations of different species of fish painted in many colours (Plate 34). They are superb examples of the X-ray style. Included also is a small number of paintings of turtles, kangaroos and other food animals.

The shelter itself is lofty and 'cathedral-like' (Plate 14 bottom), with a great overhang of rock which forms a protective roof over the painted walls. The art is afforded added protection by a high natural ledge of rock which prevents animals from rubbing against the wall. Wasps have contributed slight damage to some paintings by building their nests over the designs.

There is another extensive frieze of paintings on a flat, smooth face on the back wall of an open shelter opposite the main Obiri gallery (Plate 15). This composition depicts a series of men in motion, running across the wall. From left to right, the first man is running; he has ornaments on his elbows, a bag hanging from his shoulder, a goose-wing fan, a spear in one hand, and a small spear-thrower in the other. The second figure is about to launch a barbed spear. He is carrying a goose-wing fan and two long-bladed spears. The third man has arm ornaments and a long string bag hanging from his shoulder. He is carrying a short-barbed spear at the level of his body. The fourth figure is in a running position, with a single-barbed spear and spear-thrower in one hand and three multi-barbed spears in the other. He has a head-dress and a carrying-bag hanging from his shoulder. The fifth figure is also running. In one hand he is carrying a small spear and a spear-thrower while in the other he has a goose-wing fan and three multi-barbed spears. He also has arm ornaments and a long carrying-bag. The sixth man is standing with the sole of one foot resting against his knee. He carries a spear and spear-thrower in one hand. An arm ornament hangs from his elbow and a goose-wing fan from the forearm. The seventh and last man is in a running position. He also has a spear and spear-thrower in one hand, barbed spears in the other, and a long carrying-bag hanging from his shoulder.

In the extreme right of the gallery is a freshwater tortoise, in X-ray art. In the centre of the frieze are two long-bodied triangular-faced *Namarakain* women who have been painted over the running men. Between their fingers the *Namarakain* women are holding the loop of string by means of which they travel from place to place during the hours of darkness.

Mountford (1956: 166) adds: 'The fertility of design in the frieze of the running men is surprising. Each figure differs from the others in outline, in decorations and in the arrangement of the weapons.'

This painted scene was recorded by Mountford in 1949 and re-photographed by Edwards in 1973. Plate 15 compares the two records and shows that some slight re-touching of the designs may have taken place during the intervening period.

These paintings also are comparatively well-protected and provide an excellent record of the large animated figurative art found at many sites in the Alligator Rivers Region. Often such paintings are in an advanced state of deterioration.

On the rocky outcrops comprising this site, there are many paintings of fish and other animals in X-ray style. These are in

general well-preserved and well-protected and add to the important body of art in this area. There are also figures of Europeans with guns painted in red ochre. Another interesting detail is an Archer fish blowing droplets of water from its mouth to knock down an insect for food.

One of the sites at Obiri is situated on a large boulder a short distance from the other sites. The best depiction of a spider known to date in Aboriginal art has been painted in this gallery but exposure to weathering, in particular water running back from the drip-line, is gradually destroying the whole of the art (Plate 38 top left).

The survey of three hundred sites during the Alligator Rivers Region Environmental Fact Finding Study, has enabled positive assessment of each site in relation to others in the region. It can be stated firmly that the Obiri paintings are some of the best examples of Aboriginal art in Arnhem Land and among the best in Australia. In international terms, they rate with the great Palaeolithic art sites of France and Spain and the Bushmen paintings of Africa.

The outstanding composition of the art, the clustering of many sites in a limited area, ready access and the natural protection afforded the paintings by extensive rock overhangs, makes this area ideal for cultural tourist development. Buses already visit Obiri along a dusty track which passes between the main galleries (Plate 43 bottom). It is inevitable that dust rises with the passing of each vehicle; this drifts into the shelters and on to the painted walls.

Cannon Hill-Hawk Dreaming Region

The irregular sandstone residuals of the Obiri region extend to Cannon Hill and Hawk Dreaming, where over one hundred individual galleries have been located.

An indication of the concentration of sites can be seen on Plate 13 top. Evidence of a continuous presence of Aborigines in this area can be inferred from the density of Aboriginal cultural relics, including stone arrangements, rock engravings and burial caves.

During his 1949 field study, Mountford (V. I, 1956: 170-181) recorded many of the Cannon Hill-Hawk Dreaming paintings. Styles range from the earliest to the most recent cultural paintings.

There is evidence that as late as 1920, a traditional way of life, including painting in caves, was being carried on by Aborigines at Cannon Hill. In that year, Carl Warburton and Lawrence Whittaker took up a buffalo shooting lease on the East Alligator River. While making a preliminary survey of the area they formed a base at Cannon Hill and then made trips on to the Magela Plain. Upon reaching Cannon Hill, they discovered a large cave in front of which '. . . were strewn the bones of kangaroos and other animals and the head of a crocodile with rotten meat hanging to them. Inside it was too dark to see beyond a few yards; so we gathered some dry bracken and made a torch. We entered warily, not knowing what might be lurking within.

'It was a revelation. The walls rose to about forty feet [12.1 m], and along one side was a ledge of stone . . . apparently the cave had been used for hundreds of years. There was now no sign of life.

'In the flickering light of the torch our eyes suddenly alighted upon a group of Aboriginal paintings along the side. They held us in amazement. Exceptionally life-like reproductions of kangaroos, turtles, crocodiles, emu, nude lubras with well-developed breasts, and hands, had been painted with red, yellow and white ochre. We tested the paint, but it gave no sign of smearing.

'There were also drawings and carvings. I had no idea that Aboriginal art could reach such a high level.'

As they reached the last hill before Cannon Hill, and were passing through a narrow entrance to a small valley, there appeared about thirty Aborigines fearsomely painted and armed with spears '. . . Their hair had a reddish tinge in it, through the cartilage of their noses were stuck teeth of animals, pieces of sharpened shell or carved wood and they were painted in red and white stripes across the belly and chest and down the thighs and face.'

The leader was named *Koperaki*. Warburton records that this encounter was the beginning of a friendship with *Koperaki* which lasted for many years. '. . . He was the finest type of black man I ever met. Always strictly honourable and honest . . . He used to go to Oenpelli and the old Kopalgo mission, trading beeswax and other stuff.'

Warburton (1934: 101-216) established a base at Cannon Hill and provides detailed accounts of Aboriginal life at that time and the involvement of local Aborigines in the first close contact situation with Europeans.

Hawk Dreaming

From the description, and the mention of 'carvings', it is probable that Warburton's cave was in close proximity to what is now known as 'The Small Labyrinth'. This enclosed cavern is at the northern end of a rock outlier known as Hawk Dreaming. The site consists of three narrow inter-connected chambers approximately twenty-five to thirty metres long and four metres wide. The entrance to the cavern is on the cliff-face four metres above the level of the surrounding plain. In the northern chamber a fine dusty deposit, one and a half metres deep, has accumulated. This was found to contain a small quantity of bone and a few stone artifacts. An imposing figure of a speared kangaroo has been painted on the rock-face at the entrance to the cavern (Kamminga and Allen 1973: 18, site C.H. 1).

Near this site there is a cave, the walls of which are covered with large engravings similar to the 'grinding-grooves' which have a wide Australian distribution (McCarthy 1958: 14-17). This is one of two sites of engravings in the Cannon Hill-Obiri-Hawk Dreaming area. The other site is on a flat rock in a small low cave at the eastern end of an outlier situated between Cannon Hill and the East Alligator River.

The densest concentration of sites in the Alligator Rivers Region is on Hawk Dreaming, a flat-topped mesa-like outlier, known by the *Gunwinggu* as *Gargun* or Chicken Hawk Dreaming. In some parts of the outlier huge sheets of sandstone have collapsed to form shelters which afforded the Aborigines protection from the weather. Twenty-two major sites have been located (Plate 13 top). They are situated all over this rugged hill. Some are at ground level, others are adjacent to rock ledges on hillsides while still others are in rock over-hangs near the summit. In places small groups of *Mimi* figures are out of reach on boulders protruding from cliff-faces. Many of the caves have been used for the deposit of human remains.

On the flat top of the outlier there is an extensive arrangement of stones discovered by Frank Woerle, the local ranger.

A short distance to the south-east of 'The Small Labyrinth' is a ledge of rock with a series of small open caverns at the base of the associated cliff-face (Kamminga and Allen 1973: 19, site C.H. 2). From the ledge there is a commanding view of Cannon Hill with its associated lagoons. There is an interesting series of paintings on this cliff-face. One of the principle paintings is of a human figure in white ochre, probably a representation of a European. The body is round, leg and arm muscles are shown and also facial details. Associated with this figure are stencils of hands and a tomahawk. Sailing ships feature at

71

this gallery, one is a Macassan prau, while the others are of European origin. The latest styles are in white pigment and overlay traditional X-ray, *Mimi* and other styles.

A comparison between photographs taken at this site by Mountford in 1949 and Edwards in 1973, shows that paintings in reasonably protected situations have withstood weathering over twenty-four years. On the other hand, exposed sections of the gallery have suffered badly from water erosion.

An interesting example of *Mimi* art high up on the cliff-face is a small canoe with two *Mimi* figures, one 'poling' the craft over a lagoon.

On the plain near the base of the outlier there is a group of boulders which form a small irregular-shaped shelter. On one surface there is an excellent representation of a fresh-water crayfish in red ochre. This small, precisely painted figure, is one of the finest examples of Aboriginal art located in the Cannon Hill-Hawk Dreaming area. In an adjacent part of the shelter there are other paintings, including an aeroplane which no doubt dates to the second world war.

'Cockatoo Woman Cave'

Some of the most unusual paintings of the Hawk Dreaming series were located in a small shelter formed by a number of large scattered boulders. At the entrance there is a remarkable painting of a female figure with legs and arms widely spread. Within her body are small male and female figures painted in modified X-ray. Another curious human figure, in red and white ochres, has a body made up of con-centric circles (Plate 10 top right). Other paintings in the gallery include stencil arms and hands, X-ray fish and hunting figures.

On another rock surface there is a number of attractive and un-usual paintings thought to be self-portraits of *Mimi* people. One of the figures has a much exaggerated penis and holds a stick in his hands. The main figure is nearly two metres high and holds two short throwing spears in the left hand. This tall, thin figure has been painted over a small, red-brown running man carrying a goose-wing fan and multi-barbed spear in his right hand.

The shelter is very damp and moulds grow on some surfaces. Water obviously flows over the floor during the wet season and some paintings have suffered badly from water which runs over parts of the walls.

There is a random pattern of cup-shaped hollows ground into the surface of a large boulder on the shelter floor.

The Big Labyrinth

There are places at Hawk Dreaming where great tunnels and hollows have been weathered into the hillside. One such complex is known as 'The Big Labyrinth'. This comprises a series of interconnecting caverns and passages about one hundred metres long, at a level five metres above the floor of a small valley on top of Hawk Dreaming. The larger caves are decorated with paintings of fish, kangaroos and human figures but their condition is very poor. Two chambers contain secondary burials (Kamminga and Allen 1973: 32).

Warlkada

A large north-east facing shelter, known as *Warlkada*, is located on the northern end of Hawk Dreaming. Rich in occupation deposits, it was excavated by White in 1965 and found to contain bones, fresh water and marine shells and stone tools (White 1967: 426-431).

A concentration of recent white ochre paintings decorates the walls and ceiling of the shelter. Stencil arms and hands in white ochre predominate. They are obviously recent as they superimpose earlier styles. A stencil of a steel axe complete with handle is unusual (Plate 12 middle left). A ship with sails, cabin and portholes, is a central figure in the gallery. There is an outline painting of a cowboy wearing a wide-brimmed hat and European clothes; the Sydney Harbour Bridge and a cat, complete the range of contact paintings.

These records trace the arrival of Europeans in the Alligator Rivers Region, from the first ships to venture up the East Alligator River, until recent times.

Mimi Art Sites

On the western side of Hawk Dreaming, there are galleries containing superb examples of traditional *Mimi* art. These sites were found first by Chaloupka (pers. comm.), during one of his frequent investigations in this region. There are sites near the base of the hill but the most impressive paintings, and best preserved, are in protected shelters high up on the hill.

One frieze of particular interest shows a battle scene with two men carrying a dead comrade on their shoulders (Plate 17 bottom). This is a well preserved excellent example of *Mimi* art. Other small figures, running with spears set in spear-throwers in readiness for launching, a row of jabirus with fish held in their beaks, women with well formed breasts, and grotesque spirit figures, all make up an outstanding gallery of *Mimi* art in natural red ochre (Plate 16).

73

Archaeological Sites

To the west of the main Hawk Dreaming outliers are several residuals. Occupation deposits in one of them, called *Nawamoyn*, were excavated by White (1967: 191-253) and found to contain relics dating back over 21 000 years. A wide range of faunal remains and stone and bone tools, were recovered from the site. The most significant finds were examples of edge-ground axes which pre-date similar tools found elsewhere in the world. Comparable dates were obtained from deposits excavated at another nearby shelter named, *Malangangerr*. A third site, *Padypady*, is located at the summit of a high, isolated rock. The excavation undertaken by White in the occupation deposits at this site, produced a range of well preserved midden material, including plant remains and wooden artifacts. The site had been occupied from 3 000 years ago until the last century. There are a few paintings at this site but their condition is poor.

Cannon Hill

The outliers in the Cannon Hill complex (Plate 18) become islands at the height of the wet season as they are isolated on extensive flats. Prolonged weathering has fashioned the soft sandstone rocks of which the outliers are composed into a maze of shelters which are so formed as to afford protection from every quarter.

The main gallery between the Cannon Hill series and the East Alligator River has a low ceiling but is quite spacious. Many figures have been painted on the ceilings and walls, including X-ray art, *Mimi* figures and a range of other designs. The most outstanding group is of several grotesque spirit figures in red and white ochres (Plate 28 bottom). A colour photograph of this ceiling frieze was published by Mountford (1954: Plate IX) who described the figures as *Namarakain*, the small thin-bodied people similar in appearance to the *Mimi*.

One gallery at the back of the main site is decorated with a large spirit figure in red ochre holding a spear-thrower in one hand. Fish in X-ray style surround the figure; near one arm is a naturalistic representation of a spider (Plate 20). This and the larger spider at Obiri Rock, are unusual as insects seldom feature in rock art.

The engravings mentioned previously cover the floor of a small shelter at the east end of the group. The ceiling of this shelter is very low and it is difficult to understand how the grooves were formed; possibly they were ritual marks rather than the result of sharpening axe-heads.

74

The Eastern Outlier

A lagoon extends from near these outcrops to the base of one of the large outliers of the main Cannon Hill complex. From the summit there is a commanding view of the East Alligator River winding its way northwards to the sea, over the vast, black soil plains, with the main escarpment in the background.

Geese, ducks, brolgas, jabirus, ibis and other water fowl frequent this lagoon. It contains also a rich supply of fish. Buffaloes graze in hundreds on the plains and across the river is the Oenpelli holding, with its great herds of cattle which flourish on the rich herbage of the flats. This environment is ideal for man and animal alike and it is not surprising that the network of caves and shelters in the hillsides near the lagoon contain obvious evidence of long Aboriginal occupation in the form of paintings, camp debris and human remains.

There are several rock shelters formed by under-cutting of the soft sandstone at the base of the hill. Paintings in these galleries have been badly damaged by buffaloes and pigs which rub against the decorated walls. During the current series of field surveys these animals were seen in the shelters, actually damaging some of the paintings.

A steep-sided gully is located at the east end of the outlier. The northern face is precipitous yet high up on the cliff there is a series of ochre paintings, visible only through binoculars. In the past a rock ledge must have existed to provide access to the face. Possibly an earth tremor caused its collapse. Evidence of earth movements and associated rock falls is provided by Warburton (1934: 79-80) who describes such an occurrence in the Cannon Hill area in 1920: 'Suddenly everything became hushed, the birds were still and the horses pulled up quivering . . . looking back [I] saw the rocks shaking like a child's wooden blocks in a wind . . . loose rocks [fell] from the cliff . . .'

On the southern side of the gully there is a ledge about half way up the wall of the gorge. This is quite wide at the eastern end but terminates at the end of the gorge. The sandstone is undercut along the margin of the ledge and weathered to form a series of caves, shelters, crevices and deep niches.

Several of the deep hollows contain human skulls and bones; evidence of their use as repositories for skeletal material at the termination of mortuary rites.

There is a large, deep cavern at the eastern end of the gorge. This shelter is about twelve metres above the level of the plain and overlooks the billabong and residuals on the plain. Kamminga and Allen

(1973: 20) examined the cave and found a substantial occupation deposit, including shells and animal bones. The existence of glass, flaked to form scrapers, a carved wooden pipe and a wire fish spear, were indications that the site had been occupied until quite recent times. Similar evidence was found in most of the shelters in the Cannon Hill-Hawk Dreaming area.

There is a number of paintings on the cliff-face adjacent to the rock shelter. They are, in the main, weathered human figures and animals. Despite the deterioration there is a wide range of designs, particularly in the *Mimi* style.

Close examination of the remainder of this outlier resulted in the location of twelve major sites, several with elaborate X-ray paintings of kangaroos, fish and other animals. Besides the main galleries numerous small groups of *Mimi* figures were found in a broad scatter over the rocks. These red ochre figures occur frequently under ledges, in crevices and on small rock-faces and depict men and women in a wide range of activities, in particular hunting and dancing. One frieze shows a ceremony with a group of performers and a seated didjeridu player. The didjeridu in *Mimi* art is evidence for an early origin for this wind instrument.

Cannon Hill itself contains several small shelters with paintings; in all there are some fifty sites located between the East Alligator River and Hawk Dreaming (Plate 18).

The Cannon Hill-Hawk Dreaming region is clearly linked with Obiri Rock sites near the East Alligator River Crossing. The region has seen intense occupation by Aborigines for well over 20 000 years. The whole area is rich in sites and lends itself to development as a living museum of Aboriginal art and culture.

Birndu (Ngarradj Warde Djobkeng — the cockatoo split the rock)

This complex of sites (Plate 21 bottom) is located over one kilometre south-east of Padypady on the western edge of a very large massif. *Gunwinggu* men told Peter Carroll that the escarpment at this point was split in the Dreamtime by the sulphur crested cockatoo.

There are four main art sites in close proximity to one another. Two large shelters have been formed by extensive weathering of the summit of a large residual, indeed it is possible to walk through the complex of large shelters and caves which form the hill-top. These would have afforded adequate accommodation for many Aborigines no matter what the weather conditions as they could move to different parts of the shelter according to the prevailing conditions.

The walls and ceilings of these two shelters are covered with paintings in a range of styles and colours. There are many spirit figures, animated *Mimi* drawings and paintings in X-ray style. Their state of preservation ranges from very poor in the exposed sections of the shelter to good where they are in well protected positions.

There is another large shelter on top of the adjacent outlier which rises above the shelters. A steep climb is necessary to ascend the hill; once on top there is a commanding view of the surrounding country-side. The distant residuals of the Cannon Hill-Hawk Dreaming complex stand out in a sea of open forest and in the distance there are vast swamp-lands with their myriads of water birds.

There is a long, deep rock shelter extending for a hundred or so metres across the hill. During the wet season a small stream runs through the shelter. This would have provided a ready supply of water for the occupants. Beneath the comparatively low ceiling there are many polychrome X-ray paintings and *Mimi* figures. Water has run back from the drip-line and damaged many of them.

An important site is located at the base of this outlier. It is an open shelter extending along the cliff and has a large area of built-up deposit. This occupation debris was excavated by Allen (Kamminga and Allen 1973: 29-36). Dating of charcoal samples provided positive evidence of continuous occupation extending back for the last 10 000 years. A range of food remains were recovered from the deposits. These included fish, tortoise, geese and crabs; tidal mud-flat shell fish, cockles and whelks and the bones of large and small marsupials. Many stone tools also were found. These provided de-tails of the life style of the successive generations who occupied the shelter over such a long span of time.

The cliff-face fronting the deposit is covered with a rich array of colourful paintings. There is an extensive battle scene with dozens of *Mimi* figures involved. A great shower of spears hovers in the air over some of the assailants.

There are two distinctive figures in white ochre of running men (Plate 10 bottom left). The main one has a spear ready to launch with a spear-thrower. He carries another spear in the other hand and also a goose-wing fan. The other figure is smaller, giving an impres-sion of perspective. The smaller figure has launched his spear but retains the spear-thrower in the launching position. Older figures underlie the present frieze. Other paintings include a giant serpent, a number of fish in X-ray style and male spirit figures in white ochre.

Unfortunately this art is obscured by a layer of dust which has blown on to it from the soft ash floor. It is evident that strong winds blow along the face of the shelter as a large part of the wall has been cut into by the abrasive effects of wind-blown sand. In places the whole surface has been removed to an average depth of eight or more centimetres.

A short distance from this site there is a further gallery extending along a ledge which runs the entire length of a cliff-face. Access to the paintings is by way of a narrow rock shelf about ten metres above ground level. Many hundreds of paintings decorate the walls of this open shelter. They are under narrow ledges and overhangs and in crevices in the rocks.

Predominant in this art is a whole range of sorcery paintings. Their prevalence is an indication of the special significance of these sites. There are many X-ray figures and *Mimi* art is also well represented. A large serpent in several colours stretches along one rock-face. Fish, kangaroos and other animals are included in this fine array of colourful paintings. The Birndu area is one of considerable importance and should be rated in an 'A' category for the purposes of preservation. It lends itself to some form of protection as the four major sites are concentrated in a confined area.

A number of small rock shelters were investigated in this general region. Most of them contained paintings but many of the figures are in an advanced stage of deterioration.

A few kilometres along the escarpment there is an unusual residual weathered into a large mushroom-shaped shelter (Plate 21 top). On the walls and ceilings of this unusual feature are several large stylized male and female figures (identical to those which adorn the main site at Nourlangie Rock), X-ray drawings of fish, kangaroos, a crocodile and other spirit figures. One human figure is dissected into pieces with every detail shown. A beeswax figure of a legenary spirit man was found on one of the rock-faces.

Although this site is of some importance the small number of well-preserved paintings makes it eligible for only a 'C' category.

Mt Brockman-Nourlangie Rock Massif

This great sandstone massif rises 185 metres above the general level of the surrounding country. It is well dissected by erosion along major joint planes and is bounded by intermittent scarps on all sides.

Fifty-five sites have been located around the base of the massif (see Map 2). There are two areas of main concentration; Mt Brockman (Plate 4 bottom) itself, which is a site of sacred significance and Nourlangie Rock (Plate 5 top) where there are numerous painted galleries.

The Mt Brockman sites are located among boulders at the base of the mountain. The most important cave to Aborigines is known locally as the *Serpent's Cave*. The main figure on the back wall of the shelter is a serpent, heavily painted in red ochre. There is evidence of ritual rubbing of the figure. The other paintings in the cave including spirit figures and kangaroos, are generally in poor condition. Beeswax figures also occur. On the floor of the cave there is a large flat boulder with many distinctive cup-shaped grinding holes on its surface (Plate 35 bottom). This interesting relic is discussed in detail in a later chapter (Kamminga and Allen 1973: 54-56, site MT.B-4).

The largest of the Mt Brockman sites is divided into three galleries which are located in caves, overhangs and crevices formed in a series of massive boulders. There are dense concentrations of painted figures (Plate 22) superimposed one upon the other in different parts of the galleries. Individual figures and small groups also occur. *Mimi* paintings predominate, in some instances they hold boomerangs and also barbed spears and spear-throwers. Among the distinctive designs are several figures with disjointed limbs. Fish and other food animals are represented. There is another of the large spirit figures with small stick figures in its stomach, similar to that found at Hawk Dreaming. Many of the figures are in red ochre although there are also polychrome paintings. Hand stencils are found also at these sites. The number of X-ray paintings is less than occur at sites to the north, while contact paintings are almost absent. Some designs have been water-washed but there are many in a good state of preservation.

The Mt Brockman galleries contain all the important art styles of the Alligator Rivers Region; several are associated with a sacred site. In some instances the Mt Brockman examples are the best of their particular style. The compact group of galleries and the mountain itself, rate an 'A' category in terms of Aboriginal cultural relics worthy of preservation.

Nourlangie Rock, on the south-western end of the main massif, is another area where there is striking evidence of long past occupation by Aborigines. Large water-holes and lagoons in the area provided a ready supply of water and food. There are many rock shelters and caves in both the main Nourlangie Rock and Little Nourlangie, a residual separated from the main rock by a large freshwater lagoon.

The most impressive gallery in this region is situated at the base of Nourlangie Rock. The paintings depict a group of stylized male and female spirit figures (Plate 23 top). The ten tall, decorative figures are surrounded by a number of polychrome paintings of legendary heroes and fish in X-ray style.

One of these figures is of a lightning man who is responsible, in the Aboriginal world, for thunder, lightning and associated storms. When he became angry he would strike the ground with his stone axes which grow from his head, arm and knee joints. He would shatter trees, frighten the *Mimi* and sometimes kill people.

The Aborigines have an intense fear of thunder and lightning. Warburton (1934: 104) describes how, at Cannon Hill, his Aboriginal companions evinced great fear during a violent thunderstorm. '. . . the thunder rolled, shaking the earth beneath us, and forked and chain lightning slashed the blackness . . . [the] blacks, jabbering in terror, had moved nearer the fire, and . . . were cringing with their heads buried in their blankets. At every clap of thunder the blacks emitted pitiful yells, and their faces, lit up by each flash of lightning, were studies of abject fear. The whites of their eyes were rolling, their teeth chattering, and their limbs trembling. A deafening crash of thunder shook us, and with a terrifying yell [the] blacks grabbed fire-sticks and disappeared into the darkness. They raced for the hills, and we could see the light from their torches bobbing about as they crept into the small caves. There they spent the remainder of the night.'

The paintings in this main gallery were re-painted about 1962-63. The ochres used were coarse and the main figures show a tendency to flake (Plate 42 bottom). The life of such art works is a factor in considering the future of sites.

The Noranda Company has erected a wooden fence in front of the main gallery. This simple structure which fits tastefully into the landscape, is effective in keeping people away from the paintings.

There are many sites, both large and small, adjacent to this main site. One gallery to the west is very large and has a lofty overhanging roof. Rifles feature on one wall and high above is an array of thin-limbed spirit figures. The later art is superimposed over X-ray style fish. There are other shelters with paintings further along the base of the hill. Grinding hollows cover the surface of rocks in some of the shelters.

Many of the caves were used as burial chambers but the skulls and most of the other remains have been stolen or destroyed.

Establishment of a safari camp at Muirella Park opened this area to visitors in the early 1960s.

Nangaloar

This large site is often referred to as the *Ship Cave*. This shelter extends for a distance of some seventy metres along the base of high cliffs. In one corner there is a trickle of spring water which provided the occupants with a ready supply of cool water.

One of the main figures in the gallery is of a sailing ship trailing a dinghy (Plate 12 top left). In white ochre, this design is well-known and has been photographed often by visitors to this impressive gallery. There is a series of finely executed X-ray fish which were painted on the main wall of the shelter about 1964 (Plate 37 bottom) and high on one face is a group of totemic beings which could have had legendary significance (Plate 24). It is tragic that no record of the real meaning of this art was made in past times when the traditions of the region were known in great detail by local Aborigines.

Dust is a hazard at this site and much of the surface is covered with a thick coating, whipped up from the dusty floor of the shelter.

The site was excavated by Allen; the relative significance of the paintings will be discussed later in this report.

Nangaloar is visited regularly during the dry season by tourist buses but steps have not been taken to safeguard the site from damage.

Besides the major sites at Nourlangie Rock there are twelve other shelters which have paintings on their walls and ceilings.

Little Nourlangie Rock

At Little Nourlangie many outcrops are honeycombed with passages, caves and shelters which have been sculptured from the soft sandstone rocks by the weather. These have been occupied and used as galleries by the Aborigines.

There are six small sites. One of particular importance is situated near the water-hole. There are male and female spirit figures painted on the western face of the boulder in blue and white pigments. The blue colouring is said to be Reckitts washing blue. The paintings are finely executed and excellent examples of their style. X-ray fish also decorate the shelter.

One painting has been identified by scientists as a relic species, the Fly River Turtle of Papua New Guinea, of which one specimen was found in the Daly River area of Northern Territory in 1969 and one found in the region during the current study. Except for the Aboriginal painting, this is the only Australian record of this species (Plate 25). Most of the paintings are well preserved but there is one large crocodile in X-ray style which has suffered badly from water damage. Remnants of a paper-bark bed survive on the floor of this cave.

Two small niches in a large outcrop at the south end of Little Nourlangie were used as burial chambers by local Aborigines. At one time there were ten skeletons preserved at this site. All now have been stolen; the last two skulls were taken in 1973. Other bundle burials have been placed high up in crevices in an adjoining outcrop.

Excavation of deposits in a small shelter at the side of this outcrop resulted in a date of nearly 9 000 years for occupation of the area (Kamminga and Allen 1973: 64-66).

Another large shelter is located about sixty metres up on the western tip of Little Nourlangie. There is a number of paintings on the cliff-face but they are in a poor state of preservation.

Nourlangie Rock Escarpment Sites

Other shelters with paintings and occupation debris are situated along the base of the main Nourlangie Rock escarpment. One shelter of importance is located high up on the hillside. From this position there is a commanding view of the main Arnhem Land escarpment (Plate 26 bottom).

The paintings on the ceiling and back wall of the shelter include spirit figures and a range of animals. However, they are badly weathered and some of the most important paintings have been damaged by water which runs back from the drip-line during the wet season (Plate 26 bottom).

Paintings in other sites along the base of the escarpment are in most instances neither distinctive nor well preserved.

Djerlandjal Rock

A small compact shelter situated south of Mt Brockman and adjacent to the main access road to Koongarra contains a gallery of well preserved paintings. The main figure is of a hunter (Plate 27 top). In one hand he holds a spear mounted in a spear-thrower and in the other a bundle of small goose spears, identical to those described by Leichhardt (See page 14). Both male and female figures are painted in a range positions and activities. There is a large amount of superimposition, with X-ray style paintings of fish clearly visible beneath the more recent art works. Numerous other painted figures decorate the back wall of the shelter. These are among the best preserved paintings in the Alligator Rivers Region and have been given an 'A' category.

There is another small site on a nearby rock-face where a large X-ray style catfish, a turtle, sailing ship and domesticated animals, including a goat, have been painted on the back wall together with hand stencils and several lines of wax pellets which underly the fish.

Nearby there is a painting of a kangaroo-headed snake identified by Aborigines as a 'Rainbow Serpent', one of the most important legendary beings in Australian mythology with a distribution throughout the continent. The figure is painted in dark red, and is in the oldest tradition of painting in Arnhem Land.

On the summit of the main Djerlandjal Rock there are two large caves, both some fifty metres in extent. At the entrance to the shelters there is a whole range of ochre paintings. X-ray designs are common, with fish and kangaroos predominating. Spirit figures, an excellent stencil of a boomerang and a number of hands, make up an interesting array of art. One of the paintings has been pounded with a hammer-stone. The paintings are moderately well preserved; the best being in monochrome red.

There are many signs of prolonged occupation in these shelters and there is no doubt that one of them would warrant systematic excavation.

Development of Nourlangie Area

The Nourlangie Rock area (Plate 5 top) is close to the main Arnhem Land highway. With its picturesque topographical features, water-holes and concentrations of Aboriginal paintings and sites, it is a region where preservation of cultural sites could be achieved through controlled tourism.

The Main Escarpment

There are some seventy sites situated along the base of the main escarpment between the East Alligator River Crossing and the entrance to Deaf Adder Creek Valley (See Map 2). A number of these sites were located during a close examination of many kilometres of the escarpment and others were found by geologists. Most of the occurrences are comparatively minor with few paintings, often in a poor state of preservation.

A major site of significance is at Sawcut (Hickey) Creek where both paintings and prehistoric rock engravings were found. As this site is sacred it will be discussed later in the report.

There is a number of major sites in outliers near the East Alligator River Crossing. Residual outcrops scattered amongst the open forests contain sites with paintings. One of the main galleries figures a series of interesting designs. There is a figure of a hunter running with a decorated spear-thrower in one hand and in the other a dead goose painted in X-ray style and three spears. This painting is super-imposed upon earlier X-ray paintings of large fish.

In the same gallery there is a remarkable series of hunters in white ochre. One is about to fall to the ground as he has been speared by five barbed spears. Three men are running away from the dying hunter carrying spear-throwers but no spears. Despite the good condition of many of the figures considerable damage has occurred to some paintings. Water has washed over some faces and wasp nests cover large areas (Plate 38 bottom right). However, this shelter is one which contains sufficient well-preserved and distinctive designs to warrant an 'A' classification.

Deaf Adder Creek Valley

One of the main watercourses draining the western Arnhem Land Plateau is Deaf Adder Creek. It reaches the plain by way of an extensive valley and joins Nourlangie Creek, a tributary of the South Alligator River.

Deaf Adder Creek Valley lies south-west of the upper reaches of the East Alligator River and extends in a south-west direction for nearly fifty kilometres. The river valley varies in width; in the western region it is about eight kilometres wide and narrows towards the central region where at some points it is only a hundred or so metres wide. The narrowest point is at the 'Island' where it is almost blocked by a rock massif. The cliffs along the creek are highest in the west. In the east they flatten out to an undulating boulder-strewn plain.

Major sources of permanent water are located in the western and central portions of the valley and there is a plentiful supply of fish, water-birds and game. Clustered around the permanent waters are extensive galleries of rock art.

The existence of rock paintings in the western-most region of the Deaf Adder Creek Valley has been known since 1962-1963. Brandl (1973: 1-2) was the first to record the extent of Deaf Adder Creek sites in the valley and the escarpment to the north and south. Intrigued by Mountford's statement about the likely existence of rock painting sites along the Arnhem Land escarpment, beyond the concentrations at Obiri Rock and Cannon Hill, Brandl set out in 1968 to investigate the area on foot. He also made later visits to record and study the initial discoveries.

Subsequently Lindner and Chaloupka, have made further finds in the area and during the Alligator Rivers Region Environmental Fact Finding Study several small galleries were located and an excavation carried out at one of the main sites. This produced important evidence on the antiquity of Aboriginal occupation in the region. A total of ninety sites have been located in the Deaf Adder Creek Valley.

The region is unique as to the number of sites in a well defined area. Designs range from early style red ochre paintings to *Mimi* and X-ray art. Contact paintings are less in evidence than at Cannon Hill, Obiri, Oenpelli and other sites to the north. The most important aspect of art is the large number of mytho-totemic designs which express, in a highly sophisticated manner, the relationship between man and nature—a central concept of Aboriginal religion. Many of these designs are unique in Aboriginal rock art, for instance, the 'Kangaroo Men', mythical beings in human shape with the head of a kangaroo and holding or throwing weapons, the 'yam people'

Plate 24 Colourful spirit figures at the Nangaloar gallery near Nourlangie Rock. These paintings are believed to have been of special significance to Aborigines of the region. Archaeological excavations of the cave floor deposits provided evidence of only recent occupation.

depicted in human form and also representations of the 'Rainbow Serpent' as a kangaroo-headed snake or sometimes incorporating human and animal characteristics or in almost completely human shape. As in Aboriginal mythology, the Rainbow is sometimes depicted at Deaf Adder Creek Valley sites as a bi-sexual being (Brandl 1973: 181).

Kolondjarluk Creek Sites

One of the main concentrations of sites is associated with a large permanent lagoon (*Djuwarr*) formed at the entrance to the gorge of the Kolondjarluk Creek. Rock art sites extend along the escarpment to east of the main lagoon. A rock shelf, formed at the top of a talus, provided access to the cliff-face where there are shelters formed by the under-cutting of the rocks. The walls are covered with a range of colourful painted designs for a distance of some fifty metres. The main figure is a long snake in X-ray style. It is surrounded by fish, also in X-ray style, painted hands and female spirit figures, similar to those at the main Nourlangie site and found also on the plateau and as far distant as Sleisbeck on the upper reaches of the Katherine River. Besides X-ray paintings there are many animated *Mimi* figures depicted as hunters and also participating in many other activities. There is a painting of a four legged animal identified by Nipper Gabarigi as a native cat.

This site is important as it provides a representative selection of the main styles found in the Alligator Rivers Region. Most of the paintings are well preserved as they are protected by the overhang of the cliffs (Kamminga and Allen 1973: 94, site D.A-3).

Boulders at the base of the talus also contain paintings; several beeswax figures were found at these sites.

Sites to the West of the Lagoon

To the west of the lagoon there are numerous boulders which have fallen from the cliffs and come to rest near their base. Many of these have been weathered into shelters and there are obvious signs of Aboriginal occupation. Rock paintings feature in many shelters; in some, edge-ground axe-heads were found on the floor where the Aborigines had left them.

In one shelter there is an interesting series of echidnas painted in X-ray style. Spines have been drawn on the outline of the body and the backbone and internal organs are shown in great detail. Red and white ochres have been used to paint these excellent figures. On the same rock-face there is a series of fish in X-ray style and a number of representations of vulvae.

86

One of these sites, known as the *Lindner Site*, was excavated by Kamminga and a radiocarbon sample from the depth interval 170-190 centimetres gave an age of about 19 000 years. Recovery of 7 722 stone implements from this cave deposit is evidence for prolonged and concentrated occupation of this area (Kamminga and Allen 1973: 95-98).

The Gorge Sites

A short distance up the gorge from the lagoon, another valley leads off to the east. There is a number of paintings in a fifty metre long shelter at the base of high cliffs. Discarded quartzite flakes lie about on the floor, providing evidence of tool making at this site.

Small groups of paintings were found under ledges and on rock walls right up the rugged gorge, almost to its limit where a waterfall blocks the way.

Balawuru Site

The most extensive gallery of X-ray art in the Deaf Adder Creek Valley is known as *Balawuru*. It is reached by following the eastern-most flood channel of Balawuru Creek towards the entrance to the gorge. A high wall runs in a south-west/north-east direction. The base is smooth and paintings extend for some forty metres along the cliff. At the southern end there is a vertical cleft in the rock from which vines grow and spread over the paintings. Some fifteen metres above ground level the cliff projects slightly, along its full length. This ledge, together with a slight inclination outwards of the main wall, gives some protection to the painted gallery. The direct sunlight reaches the paintings about noon each day and it is these conditions that cause some flaking of the pigments. Buffaloes had access to the site until a strong protective fence was erected in 1972.

The gallery and its environment are most impressive. Superimposed paintings in many colours cover the whole length of the rock-face and continue up the wall for two and a half metres to four metres. Brandl (1972: 16-17) states 'the most striking paintings . . . are large-scale designs of human and animals in X-ray representation, executed in elaborate technique' (Plate 29) '. . . the clearly discernible designs number, in round figures, eighty human and 150 animals, about ninety of which depict fishes; but there are probably some one hundred others, faded designs and details that would merit inspection and recording.'

Included in the great mass of paintings is one of a man holding a rifle. It is interesting to note that he holds this in the same way as an Aboriginal holds a spear in the thrower. Another main figure is of a woman dressed for food gathering with a basket suspended from her head. There is also a painting in white of a didjeridu player (Plate 30).

A striking painting is set in a recess in the cliff above a fresh-water spring. An Aboriginal described it as a 'bird' or 'owl' man. In addition to wings, the creature has arms and hands. The head is not unlike that of an owl, but the radiating lines surrounding it are often found in paintings of mythical beings (Plate 10 top left).

An interesting feature of the gallery is the existence of numerous cup-shaped depressions which have been hammered into the surface of the walls. These are obviously man-made; all have been painted over by layers of paintings. It seems highly possible that the 'engravings' were associated with some form of ritual that ceased prior to the galleries being used for painting (Plate 29 middle right).

Brandl made a detailed study of this site and traced the change in the conventions of style. He found that the distinction made by a *Djauan* man, regarding the paintings at Deaf Adder Creek, was that the *Djauan* people had painted and 'understood' X-ray art, but all paintings in monochrome-red, were believed to have been the work of *Mimi* people or *Mimi* spirits. Brandl noted that almost all *Mimi* figures at Deaf Adder Creek are male, with their primary sex characteristics only rarely indicated. This differs from the Oenpelli/Red Lily Lagoon area where female *Mimi* figures, and the indication of the male sex, are more frequently found. It was noted also that there are several instances of Oenpelli type and Deaf Adder Creek type *Mimi* styles in superimposition, the latter consistently belongs to the lower-earlier stratum.

The other art form at Deaf Adder Creek Valley is the X-ray style of painting. *Mimi* figures are painted in monochrome but two or more colours are used for X-ray paintings. Animals predominate in the designs, with fish and kangaroos being the most numerous. It is of interest to note that there are also paintings of humans in X-ray style.

In considering the condition and age of paintings, Brandl noted that most X-ray designs are painted on a coloured ground of comparatively coarse-grained clay pigments which does not enter the rock pores to any extent. The white and yellow base therefore disintegrates easily and with it the X-ray designs. In contrast to this the fine-grained red ochre of *Mimi* paintings appears to be long lasting. On certain types of rock this pigment penetrates the surface

88

to a depth of four millimetres or even more. Such a painting can resist weather and wind erosion and may be preserved for centuries.

An excavation trench sunk at the base of the main gallery which is about twenty metres above the valley floor, produced evidence to show that the site had been in use for 5 000 years. Stone tools found in the deposit were of the later industrial phase and included uniface and biface points. Although no paintings or rock poundings extended below floor level, ochre pieces were found in all levels (Kamminga and Allen 1973: 86-92).

The Island Sites

There are several sites opposite the 'Island'. At one of these, paintings are situated along the base of an orange coloured wall that extends over some 150 metres. As at other sites in the Deaf Adder Creek Valley, paintings in several shades of red are predominant. In addition to a large number of hand stencils there are three rows of hand prints in red ochre. There are also numerous animals and human figures painted in red. To these have been added more recent paintings of human forms painted in full white. Water, weathering and termite damage is evident at this site. In another shelter there are three crudely painted human beings in red ochre.

Mt Gilruth Sites

Mt Gilruth is located north-west of the 'Island'. It is a mountain of solid rock rising from the plateau. There is a very extensive site of rock art at the bottom of the drop. Over 200 metres of wall is covered with paintings which are predominantly red *Mimi* and associated art. There are very few drawings at Mt Gilruth which could be termed X-ray in style. Two other open shelters with paintings on the walls and ceilings are located at the base of the mountain (Plate 31 top). The main designs are kangaroos, human figures and fish, mainly painted in red ochre. They have the appearance of great age and belong to the earliest rock art tradition in Arnhem Land. Their state of preservation ranges from poor to good (Plate 31 bottom).

It is at Mt Gilruth that Brandl (1973: 195) has found a painting which bears a striking resemblance to the Tasmanian or marsupial

90

wolf or tiger (*Thylacinus cyanocephalus*). The painting, in very faded orange-red lines, is depicted as a female with the pouch opening towards the back as it is in reality. Characteristic features are the stripes down the rump and the broad base to the tail. The animal is generally dog-like in attitude, but the tail extends horizontally from the body. Brandl (1972: 24-30) has identified a number of paintings as Tasmanian Tigers. All are apparently of some considerable age as they are drawn in monochrome red ochre. It may be that these paintings of an animal not known from live specimens, or as fossils in northern Australia, do themselves indicate great antiquity for many of the paintings in the Alligator Rivers Region.

Chaloupka (1973: Rep. N.T. Mus.) has recorded a series of important dynamic figures at two sites situated near the gorge and waterholes of Djuwarr Creek, a tributary of the Deaf Adder Creek.

The figures, both male and female, have been painted in fine lines of red ochre. The fluency of line and inventiveness of design suggests a consummate and skilful artist. The brushes used may have been fine feathers or hair brushes.

Sexual organs are clearly defined and the figures filled in with fine lines, strokes and dots. The heads of the figures are covered with huge headdresses. Boomerangs multi-barbed spears and other weapons form part of the compositions. Brandl (1973: 172-173) records this style as being *Early Mimi* art.

The eastern region extending between the 'Island' and the Deaf Adder Creek-East Alligator River water-shed is a valley of hills with igneous rock outcrops. This area contains the least number of sites, however, there is an unusual feature noted by Brandl; 'the "Thunder Man" is figured in one cave with stone axes attached to head and knees.' This site is in close proximity to five others located above the waterfall at a point where Deaf Adder Creek enters the valley from the escarpment. One of these sites lies in the catchment area of the East Alligator River. Motifs of this art are comparable to those of the other regions e.g. kangaroos and human forms in motion. Many of the paintings are faded and in poor condition.

Pigments used in Deaf Adder Creek Art

Brandl discussed with an Aboriginal informant, the pigments used for the Deaf Adder paintings. The main pigments are as follows:

'White—*barndja*. The material is pipe clay which is collected as pebbles or powder, or taken as a paste from beds of the mineral in the banks of creeks or waterholes.

'Black—*djari*(*t*). This is charcoal which is used as a dry pigment or ground or mixed with water or vegetable juice as a binder.

'Yellow—*keleri*. This bright yellow pigment (limonite oxide) is found as pebbles or as a paste in or near water. Several hollows made by buffaloes in the moist ground of the creek bank between the "Island" and the waterfall were filled with this mineral.

'Red—*anngolkdjolang* or *andjolang*. This is a general term for red colour; it also means (completely) cooked food. Within the colour red, two shades are distinguished: bright-red—*worang* and dark-red—(*an*)*guraitj*.'

Aboriginal Occupation

Brandl (1972: 1-2) considers that 'Aboriginal occupation of the Deaf Adder Creek area in terms of regular, if intermittent and possibly seasonal, visits to the valley and the escarpment to the north and south of it, seems to have ceased some 60-90 years ago. That is around 1900. From 1900 on, until about 1950, the area was repeatedly visited, mainly by the members of the *Djauan* tribe (*aledburrit* division), but increasingly also by *Gunwinggu* (*Maielli*) people who came from the Mudginbarry/Oenpelli area.

'Up to about 1900, and more so in the distant past, Deaf Adder Creek seems to have been a centre of Aboriginal activity of both ritual and more mundane nature. To this testify extensive quarries for stone implements and numerous and equally extensive painted sites. Some of the paintings are in styles and employ techniques that have, so far, not been reported from other parts of Arnhem Land.

'It was found that while there are Aboriginal sites in both the valley and the escarpment, regular visits to and travel across the latter may have ceased more than 100 years ago. There is a marked

94

difference between art styles in the valley and those in the escarpment, implying a greater age for the latter.'

It is interesting that no Aboriginal burial ground or any human bones were found in the area investigated.

Brandl found that 'while the assistance of the Aboriginal informant was valuable in a general way and in the identification of subjects in the paintings, only limited information could be obtained regarding the interpretation of motifs in terms of Aboriginal mythology. This is due mainly to the age of the paintings; the practice of painting on rock as a social and cultural activity ceased apparently earlier at Deaf Adder Creek than was the case in some other parts of Arnhem Land.'

Recognition of the importance of the great number of Aboriginal art and archaeological sites located in the Deaf Adder Creek Valley led to declaration of the region as a Mining Reserve (No. 338) under the *Northern Territory Mining Ordinance, 1969-1972.* It has also become a Fauna Sanctuary. No attempt has been made to bring the sites under the *Native and Historical Objects and Areas Preservation Ordinance 1955-1961.*

The presence of some ninety sites, among them some of the most significant in Australia, and the dating of Aboriginal occupation in the Valley to over 19 000 years, singles Deaf Adder Creek out for special consideration as some form of scientific reserve. Its late discovery and difficulty of access, has protected its features and sites from interference; adequate protective safeguards should be considered in any plans for increased access to the area.

Jim Jim Creek

The frequency of major sites appears to decrease south of Deaf Adder Creek Valley. Several small shelters occur along the base of the main escarpment and there is a cluster of sites near Jim Jim Falls.

One of these sites known as 'Pandanus Snake Dreaming,' is situated north-west of the falls and contains only a few poorly preserved paintings.

97

Above the falls there is a series of sites in the vicinity of large permanent water-holes which extend back some six kilometres on to the plateau above Jim Jim Falls (Plate 32 bottom).

The sites are situated in rock shelters formed in residual outcrops of sandstone which provided smooth surfaces for painting. The designs are in the main painted in red and white ochre (Plate 32 top) and are of simple X-ray designs. Most paintings are in an advanced state of deterioration; in some places walls are flaking taking the paintings with them.

The Jim Jim Region is not a highly significant art area compared with Deaf Adder Creek, Nourlangie Rock, Cannon Hill, Hawk Dreaming, Obiri Rock, Oenpelli and parts of the Arnhem Land Reserve.

The Plateau

The Arnhem Land Plateau is an extensive dissected land mass some 200 metres above the vast plains which extend to the north coast. The soft sandstone rocks of which the major part of the plateau is composed, have been weathered to an advanced degree. Drainage has concentrated along fault lines to erode away vast ravines and steep-sided gorges (Plate 6 top). The rocks have been sculptured by the weather into fantastic shapes to form an unusual and picturesque landscape.

There are many permanent water-holes along the streams draining the plateau. Summer monsoonal rains turn these rivers into raging torrents which cascade over the escarpment in numerous water-falls.

Many hard residuals of indurated sandstone and quartzite are scattered at random over the plateau. Weathering and the collapse of great slabs of rock along horizontal bedding planes have given rise to many rock shelters. In common with those along the base of the escarpment they range in size from small to very large.

There is an adequate supply of food on the plateau. Associated with the streams and water-holes are fish, tortoise, crocodiles and water-fowl while the open rocky flats and hills are frequented by snakes, pythons, lizards and rock wallabies. The plateau formed part of the hunting ground of local Aboriginal groups who ranged over the area during the wet when the rich flats were inundated with water draining from the plateau.

The Aborigines sought protection in the rock shelters where they painted totemic and other designs on the walls and ceilings. Motifs are similar to those at the main sites along the base of the escarpment but they are neither so numerous nor so extensive. Food animals

98

feature in the galleries, while human figures and abstract designs also are painted. Black, red, white and yellow pigments were used. The impression, based on present knowledge, is that there is a preponderance of red ochre designs in the earliest styles while the later polychrome art is present only to a limited extent.

There are only a few sites known with impressive concentrations of paintings. One of the most important was found due east of Mt Gilruth by a team of geologists. The paintings at this site are in an excellent state of preservation. Massed on the walls and ceiling of the shelter, they appear fresh and vital as though the Aboriginal artists had only recently completed their work.

A rich array of polychrome art, including several spirit figures similar to those which feature at the main Nourlangie site, is superimposed upon early style paintings. Many species of fish in X-ray style predominate while a number of interesting and carefully executed paintings add to the general complexity of this fine gallery of art. Guns of different types and steel axes have been painted with great care and precision.

Fortunately this site is difficult of access and the main body of art is in a well protected situation. Providing the location is kept confidential these paintings should be preserved for many decades. This gallery is quite outstanding in relation to many other sites in the Alligator Rivers Region and can be placed in an 'A' category.

Because of the inaccessibility of the plateau there is little evidence of visits by non-Aborigines. The likelihood of interference and damage through human agencies is very slight as access is limited in some places to helicopters. The area has been investigated only to a very limited extent for the purpose of this report. There is an obvious need to extend detailed site surveys on to the plateau at the earliest opportunity.

Density of Art Sites

There is a dense concentration of rock art sites in the Alligator Rivers Region. They range in size from small to large; the condition of the paintings also varies tremendously. Clusters of sites at the Deaf Adder Creek Valley, the Nourlangie-Mt Brockman massif, Obiri Rock, Hawk Dreaming, Cannon Hill, Oenpelli and on the Arnhem Land Reserve are of special importance to Australian prehistory and generally to the study of the art of hunting and gathering societies throughout the world.

Plate 30 Detail of the main gallery at Deaf Adder Creek showing superimposed polychrome paintings. The natural colour of the rock face is visible only high up on the wall. A didjeridu player can be seen at the top of the photograph and lower down there is a group of female figures surrounded by a range of fish in meticulously hatched X-ray style.

100

CHAPTER 3

Significance of Rock Paintings

Detailed knowledge of the vast number of art sites in the Alligator Rivers Region is lacking due to absence of professional anthropological studies in this isolated region and to the disastrous impact of European contact on the original *Kakadu* inhabitants.

It is known from information supplied by Aboriginal informants, that each site originally had a name and belonged to a particular Aboriginal group which had rights of occupation and a responsibility for maintenance of the paintings and ceremonial associated with specific sites.

The colourful ochre paintings found in profusion in this region played an important part in the religious and daily life of the Aborigines. Some sacred sites feature representations of legendary heroes and were the scenes of regular rituals; other paintings on the walls of wet weather occupation shelters, were painted for a variety of reasons.

In the former instance there is associated mythology, making the figures permanent manifestations of the Aboriginal Dreaming. But, even where only natural species, or hunting and fishing scenes are represented, it cannot be simply concluded that they were drawn for pleasure, to while away the time, or to record a past occurrence. The reference may be to the future, or to both the past and the future. It has been suggested that painting fish, birds, animals, or reptiles may express the Aborigines' desire for success in the hunt, and also his belief that drawing the picture gives certainty, and even a power over the creature sought. A man sees a fine fish in the river; he paints it in a gallery, and then is certain he will see it again and spear it.

The hunter did not always succeed despite his skill with the spear and his stratagems in pursuit. The fisherman, too, sometimes failed with spear, hook or net and on occasions neither animal nor plant food could be found because of seasonal failures. Such inadequacies, whether in supply or in the chase, demanded an explanation, for they had to be prevented or forestalled; the explanation lay often in the sphere of ritual, magic and religion.

Throughout the Alligator Rivers Region there are many galleries in which most available surfaces are covered with figures. Designs are also painted in a mass one upon the other. In some instances the important thing may have been the act of painting while super-imposition could have reinforced the 'power' of the totemic beings whose images were painted so carefully on the walls of the rock shelters. The painter expressed himself, his desire and his belief. His paintings now form a comprehensive record of a past way of life which persisted for many thousands of years.

Interpretations of Rock Art

There is nothing in the known mythology, beliefs and values of Aborigines to lead us to suppose that the significance of many rock paintings differs in general meaning throughout the continent. It may be inferred that those in regions in which Aborigines had died out before they were studied have somewhat similar significance (Elkin 1964: 15).

Some anthropologists believe the Aborigines adhered to a philosophy which saw a personal or spiritual relationship between man and nature. Elkin, Berndt & Berndt, (1950: 2-3) state, 'to trail the kangaroo is not enough; it is necessary so to influence it that it will stand within range. To aim at the fish will not in itself ensure accuracy. It must be drawn to the spear of the fisherman. For such purposes, charms, rites, paintings and sacred objects are employed. So, too, man does not just wait for nature and its species to bring forth in due season. He performs rites, giving his own energy, pouring his blood on symbols of the species, and expressing his desire and need by action and chant, by decoration of his own body, and by painting or engraving sacred symbols or galleries. For the time being he becomes the hero or ancestor, or he is in the presence of the 'god' who made the tribal world what it is. By re-enacting what the ancestor or great being did, he becomes a life-giver too, therefore, nature will be productive and food-species multiply. Thus, man does his part. It is effective because he and animals and plants and natural phenomena, both in the past and present, belong to one great moral or social order, each depending on the other—man's duty being ritual, nature's being food-producing. If man is remiss, nature will fail.'

Some paintings were of special religious importance and the belief was widespread among Aborigines that sacred paintings were representations of legendary 'heroes' of their Dreamtime. The first examples of such paintings were said to have been made by the mythological ancestors themselves. These great spirit beings are credited with the creation of the homeland of the Aborigines and set the pattern of their lives. At the completion of their earthly tasks they painted their own images on the walls of rock shelters before returning to the spirit world.

Berndt & Berndt (1964: 334-335) found during their long-term studies in Arnhem Land, that rock shelters with ochre paintings were in the main increase centres, a focus of tribal religion and ritual action. They state: 'They are more than mere pictures: they represent the very essence of the spirit of the beings and creatures depicted. In the caves are pieces of rock symbolizing parts of their bodies and the ritual act of painting or touching them up released sacred energy or power: bringing on the Wet, sending out spirit children, or spirits of edible plants and natural species.'

The existence of sacred paintings was noted by a number of observers, including Rev. J. R. B. Love who visited the Kimberley area of Western Australia in 1914-15 and later became one of the pioneer missionaries at Kunmunya (1927 to 1940). Love (1936: 22-24) provided interesting details of the distinctive Wandjina paintings of the *Worora* group: 'As long as the picture of a Wondjuna [*sic*] remains in a cave, rain will continue to fall in that locality at the proper time of the year.

'The men periodically re-paint the pictures, but none will admit having been the original artist. The explanation given as to how the pictures got there in the first place is that the Wondjuna painted them, and left his own pictures behind him.

'. . . Woodoonmoi told me he had repainted the big picture of the crocodile. This is the crocodile which is supposed to live in the pool of the Glenelg, which Indamoi would not go near, though Woodoonmoi approached it gingerly.

'I learnt later that all the people know of the localities of these pictures, and that the children too know what they contain, though the children and women would not likely visit them, and none but men, elders of the tribe, have anything to do with the re-painting of the picture. The office of artist is not any sacred office, but the work may be done, secretly, by a man who may otherwise appear of no special importance in the tribe. A man does not paint pictures in his own country, but only in the territory of his mother's brother.'

Elkin (1938: 224) confirmed the interpretations of Love. He found that when a painting was touched up by men of the totemic territorial clan, rain would fall and the spirit children who come from the rainbow-spirit and sojourn in water-holes nearby, would be available for incarnation. Likewise if the men painted or re-painted representations of their totemic species on the gallery which was dedicated to a Wandjina, the species would increase. In one part of the northern Kimberleys the man who finds a spirit child must go to the gallery and touch up the painting of the rainbow serpent, and even paint a representation of a spirit child, so that the former would be able to keep up the supply. Painting and retouching them was efficacious because they were *ungud*; that is, because they were instituted in a past creative period, the 'virtue' of which can be operative today through such ritual action.

Independent studies of rock art carried out by Macintosh and Elkin at Beswick Creek Cave, south of Katherine, in the Northern Territory, provided further information on the significance of paintings to living Aborigines (Macintosh 1952: 259-261).

An informant stated that a man could go into a cave and paint a figure. When he went back to camp he would describe it to the other members of the group. Such a painting was not sacred nor necessarily esoteric; anyone could look at it, including women. If the painting represented anything sacred or secret, permission to paint it had to be obtained from the owner of that country, and furthermore, payment had to be made not only to the owner of the territory but also to the senior member of the opposite moiety. If the painting was made without first obtaining permission and without payment there was an obligation to pay an increased sum when ultimately detected.

The Aboriginal stated that after he had died, people who remembered him would go to the painting in the cave, look at it and cry for him. Subsequently, the painting would be covered with red ochre and obliterated. This action constituted an addition to the funeral rites for the man concerned. Later again another picture could be painted over the red ochre, perhaps as part of the rites associated with the final resting of his spirit.

Macintosh found two areas on the walls of the Beswick Creek Cave bearing patches of red ochre. These may have covered pictures but nothing had been superimposed on them. Again, there were three old paintings which had more recent designs superimposed on them (Macintosh 1952: 259-261).

Further evidence of the importance of rock art was obtained in 1955, when paintings of an important legendary hero were located near the abandoned mining exploration camp at the Sleisbeck on the

Upper Katherine River. The main rock shelter is situated on high ground facing down the South Alligator River Valley. There is a pathway lined with stones leading to a shelter where colourful paintings in red and white ochres cover the walls and ceiling. Initiates were said to have been led along this pathway during rituals.

Arndt (1962: 289-319) was told by Aborigines from the area that the site belonged to the *Djauan* group. The main painted figure represents *Nagorgo* (Plate 33) who was credited with having made the features of the earth, the trees, animals and the Aboriginal people. He made the ground crack, made fire come out and pushed rocks and ridges up to their present elevations.

The impressive escarpment of the Arnhem Land Plateau is said to be an example of his work. He carried a stone axe with which he made lightning and while living in the area, painted his lores on many rock-faces. Before entering the ground in the floor of the cave he painted his story and his own image on the cave walls where they have been maintained by successive generations over perhaps many thousands of years.

Some painted figures in shelters in this area are identical with those in the Alligator Rivers Region and contact between Aborigines of the two areas is certain to have occurred. Legendary stories associated with features of the landscape extend over most areas of Arnhem Land as they do in central Australia (Mountford 1968: 1-112) and elsewhere.

Nagorgo, who made lightning in the headwaters of the South Alligator River had a counter-part in *Gunwinggu* country. He was called *Namarrkon* and in rock art is depicted with stone axes at knee and elbow joints. When lightning strikes it is said to be this mythological hero striking the ground with his stone axe. His site is sixteen kilometres east of Nabarlek and consists of a portion of the escarpment face with an associated creek and a number of small hills. The area is protected under the *Native and Historical Objects and Areas Ordinance 1955-1961* (Carroll 1973: 9).

Early stylistic paintings, as well as X-ray art of food animals and images of spirit figures, are among the designs common to both regions.

Mountford (1956: 203-214) was one of the first to record legendary significance for rock art in the Alligator Rivers Region. During the 1948 American-Australian Arnhem Land Expedition he undertook extensive studies of the art and published the first comprehensive record of styles and designs.

Among the legends he recorded was one concerning the Dream-time activities of the water-snake, *Aniau-tjunu*, a mythological creature associated with Obiri Rock. The snake, with his wife and children, came from the *Matjili* lagoon, to the west of the East Alligator River, and travelled southwards until he reached Obiri, the series of residual outliers about sixteen kilometres south-west of Oenpelli. *Aniautjunu* decided that Obiri was a good place to remain. He painted his image on the walls of a cliff and with his family went inside through a crevice which opens wide enough during the night to allow the family to emerge for food gathering. Before daylight the family returns to their home and the rocks close again.

Mountford believes this site was an increase centre for water-snakes, a much favoured Aboriginal food. When the Aborigines wished to increase the supply of water-snakes in the lagoon they chose the correct season, and stood before the painting, beating it lightly with a bough to hunt out the spirits of the water-snakes and direct them to the different water-holes where they became large water-snakes. By means of this simple ritual the Aborigines believed that there would be an adequate food supply. The Aborigines with whom Mountford worked were definite that a two metre long design in yellow, with a red outline on one of the vertical faces at Obiri, was painted by the legendary water-snake, and had not been re-touched by human beings.

Mountford found the Aborigines to be particularly afraid of the spirit people *Nadubi*, whose usual habitat was in the low scrub which often surrounds the springs at the base of the Arnhem Land Plateau.

The *Nadubi*, not knowing the way to make fire, had to eat their fish and game raw. They were often so hungry that they stole the meat the Aborigines had placed in the trees over-night and the honey from their honey baskets. No Aboriginal had seen a *Nadubi*, although they had often heard them grunting in the darkness.

The *Nadubi* had barbed spines growing from their knees, their elbows, and, in the case of the women, from their vulva. When they saw an Aboriginal travelling by himself, or drinking from the springs, the *Nadubi* would sneak up behind him to shoot one of their barbed spines into his body. If it was known that the Aboriginal had been near the haunts of the *Nadubi* his friends immediately called the medicine man to remove the spine. Sometimes the medicine man succeeded, but more often the Aboriginal died. A painting of a

106

107

Nadubi was found on the roof of one of the caves at Inyalak by Mountford and re-located and recorded during the Alligator Rivers Region Environmental Fact Finding Study.

Another spirit being, *Nabarakbia* (Plate 28 bottom) of whom the Aborigines were afraid, lived in clefts of rock, or in commodious caves under banyan trees, the entrances to which were a little larger than that of a bandicoot burrow. Although his main diet was fish, *Nabarakbia* was always trying to steal the spirit of a sick man or woman by extracting it through the solar plexus. He then cooked and ate the spirit and the patient died. It was the duty of medicine men to hunt *Nabarakbia* away when they saw him loitering around the camps of sick people. A painting of this spirit in red and a little over two metres high, with his catch of fish threaded on a length of vine, is a feature on the ceiling of a cave at Obiri.

Significance of Oenpelli Art

Many paintings are said to have played a role in certain forms of sympathetic 'magic'. The first superintendent of Oenpelli Mission provided a clue to the association between art and 'magic' when he recorded how an Aboriginal named *Kanowla* explained to him that if a native misses a fish with his spear he later returns to the cave and draws in careful detail the lines in the X-ray drawing of the fish as a warning that he had better not miss next time (Dyer, 1934: 26).

Berndt & Berndt (1951: 206-209) on the basis of information supplied by a number of Aboriginal informants, recorded what they call 'art-magic' in use at Oenpelli and in the hill country to the east (Cooper Creek region) about thirty years ago. At the time the studies were undertaken its efficacy was diminishing as men of the younger generation did not paint the traditional representations that were often necessary.

The galleries of paintings recorded by Berndt and Berndt from behind Oenpelli to the mainland opposite Goulburn Island contained paintings of women with human, bird or reptile heads, several arms, accentuated breasts, and elongated vulvae; women with babes suckling at their breasts, bodies of women showing foetal growth, women dancing and men and women carrying out the sexual act. Most of the drawings were beautifully executed in red, yellow, white and black pigments, or sometimes in blood. All were on the walls and roofs of rock shelters but were found to be faded or superimposed with drawings of animals and other figures. Others again were hidden in small shelters which were almost inaccessible and could be found only with the aid of experienced elderly Aboriginal guides.

Berndt & Berndt (1951: 207-209) consider there are four types of 'magic' associated with cave paintings: '1. Drawings of individuals carrying out coitus. This is simply imitative or sympathetic magic, performed to bring about a desired situation similar to that depicted. It is said that this type of magic was employed frequently before Mission contact, and still lingers on among the older natives, who still possess the art of expressing themselves subtly in ochres on rock or bark. No concrete examples of this magic are available, except the actual drawings on the stringy-bark. In theory, this magic is said to work in the following way:

'A man desires to attract the attentions of a woman, who is not particularly anxious to have associations with him. He goes to a secluded place, either by himself or with a companion, and draws the woman in the position of coitus, and then sketches himself having coitus. He leaves this drawing, if on bark, in a protected place, and returns to the camp. That night the girl will come to his hut and awaken him, and they will go into the adjacent bush to have coitus. To retain the affection of the girl, who is usually a *'ma:mam*, the man must from time to time re-paint or touch up his drawing.

'2. Suggestive magic, which aims at causing pregnancy and facilitating coitus. There are several of these drawings in the main Oenpelli gallery behind the Gunbalanja swamp. Like the bark drawings they show a woman breast-feeding two children, one at each nipple. Another drawing shows a pregnant woman, containing a foetus, while yet another represents a woman and a child with an umbilical cord which is attached to the uterus of the mother. There are no actual cases available in which we may observe their real intent in contemporary life, but there is one story relating to the drawing of the woman breast-feeding her two children.

'3. Drawings of the third group are more plentiful, and perhaps better known. They serve as a substitute for arguments and fights which would result from a husband's jealousy or a wife's blatant infidelity, or from a woman caught in *flagrante delicto*. This is sorcery; and the aim of this destructive magic is to cause sickness and death, by drawing a likeness of the woman and calling her name. An aggrieved husband will go out secretly and draw his wife, sketching in ochres a composite figure with either an animal, reptile, bird or human head, most popular being the head of an eagle-hawk or Rainbow Snake; several arms are inserted (usually three) and stingray nails protrude from her body. When the drawing is completed, the husband calls her name; from that moment the woman begins to feel sick and after a few days dies. Again, no concrete examples were available.

'4. The last group also concerns sorcery, for the purpose of bringing sickness and death to a woman who has refused a man coitus. From the number of drawings available this seems to have been a popular form of magic at Oenpelli, but is less well-known at Goulburn Island. Actual cases are not given, but informants insisted that today it is used chiefly to force an unwilling woman to comply with a man's desire for coitus. The common phrase used is: "If you don't come into the bush with me, I'll draw you."

'One drawing represents a woman with a reptile's head, and two babies suckling at her breasts. Semen is flowing from her vagina, and stingray nails [*'mangimangi*] are sticking into her body from every direction. After the woman's name is called, her whole body begins to hurt and soon she dies. The babies at her breast symbolize that either they too will die or they will be left motherless.

'Another drawing, called *'mo:lomo:li*, shows a woman who has persistently refused the attentions of a man standing in *'ma:mam* relationship to her. The woman goes instead to another man and arouses the jealousy in the one she spurned. This can happen to a husband whose wife prefers the attentions of another lover and re-fuses to have coitus with her legal spouse. The aggrieved man makes a drawing of the woman, and calls her name. Soon she feels ill, and before long she dies.

'The whole subject of drawing in relation to magic and sorcery in this region requires close and specialized attention. The drawing man, or artist, is termed *'kabibiimbun* (he draws her), while the drawing itself is *'biribimbo:m* (they drew it), and the calling or singing of the woman's name, *'kabiwapum*. It is almost too late now to obtain detailed texts on this subject, while only a very few of the older men can draw in the traditional pattern.'

Sacred Sites at Mt Brockman

Increased activity in the Alligator Rivers Region since mineral explorations began has stimulated investigation of Aboriginal sites in areas where access in the past has been extremely difficult.

Brandl (1972: 1-25) carried out an investigation of sites located in the western part of the northern end of the Mt Brockman escarp-ment massif. According to his informants, only two sites in this country (*Namirar*) are of traditional, mytho-totemic significance: *Djidbidjidbi* and *Dadbe*.

The Aboriginal who at present shows the greatest interest in these sites is Peter Balmanidbal, *Dua, Nabaraba gunmugugur, nagodjog* subsection. He acts as spokesman for a large portion of the Abori-ginal population at Mudginbarry. He is generally accepted as the custodian of the two sites, thus succeeding the now deceased last *Namirar* custodian of the site, Paddy Gamarawu. Brandl found that Balmanidbal's authority as a ceremonial leader and his strongly traditional-oriented attitude had fitted him for the custodianship of the site. Balmanidbal himself explained and rationalised his position to Brandl by reference to the mythological era and to actual or supposed kinship ties with Paddy Gamarawu. When asked how he, a *Dua* man of *Nabaraba gunmugugur* could rightfully 'look after' mytho-totemic sites in *Jiridja Namirar* country, he gave the following explanation: 'In the beginning of time *Jingana* the rainbow made the laws, named the physical features of the country and determined the territorial affiliations of the people living there. It was *Jingana*, the Mother, who sent the *Dua Nabaraba* people into the Cadell River/ Annie Creek area, where Balmanidbal was born, near a place called *Godgululdi*, possibly on Imimba Creek which is a tributary of the Blyth River; Berndt and Berndt [1970, p. 239] list *Baraba gunmugugur* as a *Gunwinggu* fringe unit on the *Maielli* and *Dangbon* sides. Similarly, *Jingana* gave the *Namirar* territory to the people living in the Mudginbarry/Mt Brockman area. He, Balmanidbal, had now come back to his original country.'

Brandl (1972: 14) states that *Dadbe* is the more important of the two Mt Brockman sites. 'In mythical times, *Jingana* transformed the king brown snake, *Dadbu*, into the Rainbow who now lives in *Dadbe*. *Dadbu/Dadbe*, the Rainbow, belongs to the *Dua* moiety as does Balmanidbal himself and this is why Paddy Gamarawu requested that he look after the site when he [Paddy] would die.'

Djidbidjidbi and Dadbe

The north-western tip of the impressive Mt Brockman escarpment is a perpendicular cliff-face with alternating red, black and whitish vertical stains where water has flowed down the face (Plate 4 bottom). The marks are said to represent the blood of the Rainbow Snake. At the base of the escarpment there is a boulder about thirty-four metres high which has fallen from the cliffs. An area of about thirty-four metres by seventeen metres on an inclined face of the boulder has a number of faded paintings. The high cliffs and the boulder-strewn area in front of it, including the painted boulder, are called *Djidbidjidbi* — according to Balmanidbal an untranslatable place name.

On top of the cliffs and a short distance to the south-east of *Djidbidjidbi* (perhaps 180 to 280 metres) there is a rock-hole which never goes dry. This rock-hole is called *Dadbe*. It is the permanent residence of the Rainbow Snake. Aborigines insist that they have not been near the site at any time.

111

Significance of Mt Brockman Sites

On several occasions Brandl had asked Aborigines from Mudginbarry to accompany him to the paintings in the northern Mt Brockman area. The request met with refusals and excuses; they were not interested in visiting the site which, they said, was a 'Snake Dreaming place.' Aborigines camped at the East Alligator Crossing also refused, stating that they did not know anything about the paintings or that the area lay outside 'their country.' It was not until prospecting began in the area and people were noticed by the Aborigines in the vicinity of *Djidbidjidbi* and climbing into the sandstone country, that Peter Balmanidbal became concerned.

When Brandl began depth studies of the sites in May, 1972, he asked Peter Balmanidbal to accompany him to *Djidbidjidbi*. Another *Maielli* man, Fred Namijilg (*Dua, nangaridj* subsection, *Nabolmo gunmugugur*) accompanied them. Both emphasised that they had not been to *Djidbidjidbi* for a long time and never to *Dadbe* in the escarpment. When Brandl and his companions approached the first boulders near the site, both Aborigines paused and despite some twenty minutes of encouragement they refused to climb the moderate slope that leads to the cliffs. 'Perspiring profusely', says Brandl, 'Namijilg refused, saying that he did not feel well due to a heart condition and headaches. Balmanidbal showing similar signs of fear, asked me to enter the site first . . . I then climbed the slope and Balmanidbal followed after some ten minutes.' When he stood before the paintings he chanted, facing the rock wall:

> *'Ngaimeng   'ngawogdi   doidoi*
> I speak   I talk to you,   my ancestor
> *'Ngabandjaua   'ngalurgwognang*
> I have asked them   I am seeing the paintings
> *'Ngaie   andimidbun*
> They are waiting for me
> *'Wardi   'uridoweng   'ngarabolgmin*
> Maybe you are dead,   I have grown up.

The best preserved of the paintings are some fifteen motifs—mainly human figures and a few animals—in red which overlie similar motifs in yellow. Brandl says that Balmanidbal dismissed them by saying they were *'Mimi drawings'* about which he knew nothing as they had been painted by the *Mimi* spirits a long time ago. Brandl described the paintings as 'partial silhouettes' and stated that 'the main figures have animal as well as human characteristics—reptile and man—a combination of possibly totemic significance as

112

it occurs in other paintings at several locations in the Mt Brockman area' (Plate 22).

Near the base of the wall are two unusual beeswax figures depicting humans; one of them is well preserved. A double line of wax pellets is located on a rock facing the painted wall. Similar figures were found in rock shelter sites throughout the Alligator Rivers Region.

Most of the painted area is covered with polychrome X-ray art: mainly fish, humans and a crocodile, all of them in a poor state of preservation. Several thin-bodied human figures in white, some of them outlined in red, are in an equally bad state of repair.

Balmanidbal stated firmly to Brandl that none of these paintings at *Djidbidjidbi* had been done by human beings: 'It was *Jingana* the Rainbow who had put them there in mythical times.' Proof of this, for him, was that he found the picture of *Jingana* on the wall—a painting of a doubled-up snake with an animal (kangaroo) head. The particular form of the 'kangaroo-snake' he explained in the following way: 'Every snake can potentially become the Rainbow. If a snake enters a water-hole, staying close to the surface, and leaves the water when it reaches the other bank, then it will remain a snake. However, if the snake dives into the depth of the water-hole, it does so because *Jingana* the Rainbow says "You stay down here", and then the snake remains underground and becomes the Rainbow.'

Balmanidbal identified several paintings which depict females as *Ngalgunburijaimi*, the daughter of *Jingana*. *Ngalgunburijaimi*, too, is referred to as the Rainbow.

The Aborigines refused to accompany Brandl to *Dadbe* on the grounds that it was too dangerous for them to approach the water-hole. '*Dadbe*, the Rainbow, would smell them. He would come up, swallow them and destroy the country. The Mt Brockman cliffs might collapse and all the people in the area, black as well as white, would be killed.'

On the ground in front of the painted wall there are several rock slabs with many cup-shaped depressions pounded into their surfaces. These hollows occur at most sites in western Arnhem Land. One of the Mt Brockman examples, said to be the work of *Jingana*, is outstanding (Plate 35 bottom) and has been broken at some distant time in the past. Evidence of this can be seen by the advanced surface weathering of the fracture.

Spencer (1914: 334-336) found similar hollows on rock surfaces at Oenpelli. He considered them to be of great age. They were not in use at the time of his investigations in 1912. *Kakadu* informants had no knowledge of their origin and meaning; they were believed to be the work of the Thunder Man, *Namaran*, who arose at the Dreaming

Plate 32 (opposite) The top of the escarpment was accessible to Aborigines who had well used tracks to regular water and game supplies. *Top:* A weathered outcrop on the Arnhem Land Plateau, near the banks of Jim Jim Creek, six kilometres upstream from the falls. Rock paintings occur in shelters at the base of this residual. *Bottom:* Jim Jim Creek during the wet season. This extensive reach of water provided a plentiful supply of food for Aborigines crossing the plateau.

at *Lurudminni*. He sat down inside the lagoon at *Dadba* (there may be an association between this place and *Dadbe*) called *Maiigman* (lightning) by the men, though the women do not know this name. At the bottom of the pool he lived in a hole in a great rock, which is called *Nanan*. He made rain that filled the lagoon, and used to go in and out of the stone, where he camped all day. He had many spirit children with him, and lived at *Dadba* before there was any hill called *Lurudminni*; indeed, he made this and it was while attempting to open up the rock that he formed the cup-like depressions. The rock was too hard for him, so he went into the water pool again, where he kept his children, coming out every now and then to make rain and thunder and lightning.

Spencer records that the Thunder Man was a *Nakomara* man and it was only the men of this group who dared to go far into the water. The women would obtain water at the lagoon but would not bathe. During the wet season the old *Namaran* sits on top of the stone, so that half his body is under and half above water. He keeps plenty of water in the stone, and every now and then opens it and much water comes out. Then he says, 'That is good; that is plenty;' locks the stone up and the water ceases to flow.

If a *Ngaritjbellan* woman put her foot in the water, a spirit child would go up her leg and into her body; if she drank water it went in by her mouth and the child, when born, belongs to the Thunder Totem, just like the old man.

It is of interest to note that an alternative to drawing on a rock surface was stringy-bark which had to be specially prepared, smoothed and completely red-ochred to serve as a background for the drawing. A select series of these extremely important bark paintings was collected at Oenpelli from 1912 to 1914 for Sir Baldwin Spencer. They are now in the collection of the National Museum of Victoria. Berndt also made an excellent collection for the Department of Anthropology, University of Sydney.

Lightning Dreaming Site

One of the sites recently identified as being of sacred significance is 'Lightning Dreaming' near the entrance to the gorge of Hickey (Sawcut) Creek, on the main escarpment, south-east of Koongarra.

114

115

Plate 33 (opposite) *Nagorgo* an important legendary hero who made lightning, formed topographic features of the landscape and painted his image in rock shelters in the headwaters of the South Alligator River Region.

There are two large water-holes at the entrance to the picturesque gorge. Both the western one, *Didbunadjogi*, which extends about 280 metres westward of the escarpment border-line, and the eastern one, *Imurdu*, situated some distance farther upstream, are moon (*di:d*) dreaming places for Aborigines of *Kawardjag gunmugugur*. A conspicuous rock in the escarpment about one kilometre upstream from *Didbunadjogi*, is the home of *Namargon*, the Thunder Man, in his 'cheeky' manifestation. According to informants, *Didbunadjogi*, *Imurdu* and *Namargon* are dangerous (*djamun*) places which have had to be treated with great respect. It is interesting to note that this site is situated between the Lightning Dreaming sites at Nabarlek and at the headwaters of the South Alligator River. Mountford (1955: 1) gives a wide Australian distribution for lightning myths.

Prehistoric Rock Engravings

Rock engravings have been chipped into the cliff-face near the first water-hole. The engraved designs are mainly the tracks of kangaroos and wallaroos. Similar engravings are known in many parts of Australia (Edwards 1971: 363). Their distribution extends from Tasmania in the south, into South Australia, central Australia, New South Wales, Queensland and Western Australia. Detached rock fragments bearing animal tracks and also abraded grooves, were excavated in the main trench at the Ingaladdi site, south-west of Katherine. The engraved pieces were recovered between a level with an approximate depth of 1.1 m to 1.2 m dated (ANU-58) to 4 920 ± 100 BP (2 970 B.C.), and a lower level at approximately 1.7 m to 1.8 m dated (ANU-60) to 6 800 ± 270 BP (4 850 B.C.) (Polach *et al.* 1968: 187-188). As the engravings were deeply weathered and unlikely to have been executed on loose rock fragments, this age must be considered conservative. The first positive date for engravings from a systematic excavation therefore gave strong support to the circumstantial evidence for considerable antiquity of this art. Lightning Dreaming (Plate 35 top) is the main site where engravings of this type have been found in the Alligator Rivers Region. Another small group is situated at Fish Creek near Oenpelli.

An immense boulder of conglomerate rock located about one kilometre south of Lightning Dreaming contains a medium sized shelter with figures painted on the rough walls and ceiling. At this

117

point on the escarpment large columns of rock form a striking feature (Plate 36); these could have had legendary significance.

The most impressive painting at this site is a large human figure in red, white and yellow ochres (Plate 1). The paint-work is quite fresh, giving the appearance of comparatively recent re-touching. A dominant figure of this kind is likely to be a mythical hero of legendary importance. There are also many paintings of kangaroos and other food animals. The shelter is only a short distance south of a large billabong which had obviously supplied food for the Aboriginal inhabitants. There was a scatter of kangaroo and buffalo bones, pieces of tortoise shell, fresh-water mussels and land snail shells amongst the debris scattered over the floor.

Glass and metal tools were found in addition to a number of stone and wooden artifacts, including a edge-ground axe with fragments of ochre and gum adhering to it; a second axe with two fragments of its wooden handle, a shaft for a composite spear, a digging stick and discarded fragments of a didjeridu. The evidence indicated recent occupation of this shelter (Kamminga and Allen 1973: 81-82).

A bundle burial in very fine condition has been removed for safe keeping by the Northern Territory Museum.

The Archaeological Record

Where ethnographic data is lacking, the archaeological record can provide a pointer to the relative importance of rock art at some sites. In certain circumstances absence of early occupation deposits may be an indication that paintings were of sacred importance and the shelter used for ritual purposes rather than as a living site. However, this does not necessarily follow, as some shelters are unsuited to the accumulation of camp debris.

White (1969: 62) found that deposits excavated in five sites in the East Alligator River road crossing—Oenpelli region, provided overall evidence of continuous occupation for about 20 000 years up to the ethnographic present, about 100 years ago. Food remains in the deposits indicate that a wide range of flora and fauna was used by the Aborigines. They ate fresh-water and estuarine shellfish, fresh-water mussels, fish and marsupials, including bandicoots and possums. They also caught birds and water fowl. A wide range of tools made from shell, wood, bone and stone, were recovered from the sites.

Large rock shelters near Oenpelli, including Arrguluk and Inyalak, were excavated by McCarthy and Setzler (1960: 218-219) during the 1948 American-Australian Scientific Expedition to Arnhem Land. McCarthy assumed a direct connection between the occupational deposits in the floors of the rock shelters and paintings on their walls and ceilings. Most of the rock shelters excavated contained paintings or were adjacent to one or another of the extensive galleries. The paintings include a wide range of techniques and styles, such as outline drawings, silhouettes, linear figures, *Mimi* art and polychromes in the X-ray style; at *Inagurdurwil* there are also hand stencils. 'On the basis of the present evidence', McCarthy states, '. . . the mixture of stone implement traits in the deposits seems to indicate that all of these techniques of painting were practised by the natives who used the sites for habitation and for ritual drawing purposes. A study of the superimposing of the paintings in this area indicates that a succession of techniques may exist, but distinct cultural horizons could neither be determined by stratification in the deposits, nor linked with these various painting techniques or periods. The numerous examples of used pieces of red, yellow and white pigments found in the deposits, however is convincing evidence that the people who made and used the implements associated with them are also responsible for the paintings.'

The greatest depth of the deposit found by Macintosh (1952: 259-261) in the Beswick Creek cave was almost thirty centimetres; only two quartzite blades were recovered. No ochre, shells, human bones, or charcoal were present but a few odd fragments of marsupial skeletons were scattered about the floor. The evidence suggests that this particular cave was not used for continuous and prolonged human habitation.

A test trench made by Allen (Kamminga and Allen 1973: 70-72) in the Nangaloar rock shelter at Nourlangie Rock revealed a surface layer of twenty centimetres composed of dark grey sand over-laying forty-five centimetres of reddish brown sand consolidated deposit on rubble scree. Badly eroded fragments of human skull, a single tooth and some charcoal were found but no other *in situ* organic remains. A total of 414 artifacts (twenty-six identified as implements) including 116 pieces of ochre were recovered from the surface layers. It is apparent from the shallow deposit that this shelter was used for occupation only in more recent times, possibly when traditional culture was in a state of decline. Paintings of spirit figures in the cave could be of sacred significance. The large quantity of ochre found is an indication of a continuous painting tradition at this site over a long period (Plate 24).

Traditional Preservation Techniques

The need for conservation of original pigments did not concern the Aboriginal artists as continual re-touching meant that noticeable and lasting deterioration of sacred art did not occur until European

119

contact and the collapse of traditional culture. Unlike non-Aboriginal attitudes to works of art, the object was to maintain the traditional image rather than conserve the original pigments. It is only since the Aboriginal has abandoned his cave art, due to direct and indirect influences of European settlement, that advanced weathering of designs became obvious and threatened the very survival of the art. Lack of re-touching over an extended period represented a unique experience requiring new initiatives which neither Aborigines nor other Australians have as yet developed.

Tribal laws dictated that paintings had to be carefully re-touched before ritual. This was a simple procedure and a pre-requisite to any ceremony. In following this practice the Aborigines had adopted, perhaps unconsciously, an ideal procedure to ensure preservation of their ancient ancestral designs which were constantly being subjected to the forces of weathering. To change the form of sacred painted figures in any way during the process of re-touching, or to neglect their upkeep, could bring retribution on the group. Aborigines will admit to careful re-touching of sacred paintings along the original lines of the designs, and to numerous individuals undertaking this task with the permission of the owners, who are the ceremonial guardians of the sites. Gifts are made to these guardians for the privilege of painting the designs (McCarthy 1965: 65).

Elderly Aborigines of the *Walbiri* group in central Australia when taken on long journeys back to cave painting sites to which they had been introduced as young initiates, became distressed when they found the totemic designs reduced to faded images or in some instances totally weathered away. The disappearance of what was to them a highly significant part of their ancient culture came as a shock; they had neither realised that the paintings had been totally neglected for thirty to forty years nor appreciated the effects of prolonged weathering. Once a painting has suffered irreparable deterioration the attitude of the owners towards the sacred symbols may change, feeling great sadness for the ancestor concerned and appreciating the change in their whole situation, they sometimes abandon sites completely (Edwards, pers. journal, 1965-1970).

The practice of re-touching sacred art is carried on still by both the *Walbiri* and *Pitjantjatjara* groups. The re-painting of many caves as a first stage to ritual is a regular practice in central Australia. In most instances well mixed pigments were applied with a finger. Re-painting by this method is not the only way of applying pigments as there are records of the use of brushes made from sticks with the ends chewed to form bristles. Hair mounted in gum or beeswax on the end of a stick was also used.

Plate 34 Detail of fish frieze on the main wall of Obiri Rock: Two large barramundi (left) with a small eel-tailed catfish in between and alongside a large, salmon-tailed catfish. The figures were painted in polychrome X-ray style to show the external shape and internal organs. The ceiling (upper right) is infested with wasp nests which have begun to invade the painted surface.

121

The *Ngama* snake cave near Yuedumu is one of the major sites which has been preserved by regular re-painting. 'The techniques of renovation are simple' states Mountford (1968: 69), 'blocks of red ochre and white pipe-clay are ground with water on some flat stones embedded in the floor of the cave. Having loaded the base of the ball of the thumb or several fingers with the red or white ochre, the Aboriginal transfers this pigment to the broad surface of the snake design, or to the red "U"-shapes of the camps of the wild dogs. The forefinger is used to outline the main motifs in red or white pigments.'

There are records of sites being abandoned in the Kimberley region of Western Australia where Love (1930: 6-9) found Wandjina paintings nearly obliterated by rains and no longer venerated because of damage which was considered to be desecration. Several of the shelters located contained paintings in a bad state of repair. One, about three kilometres from Kunmunya Mission Station, had designs that were almost obliterated.

Love found many paintings on ceilings of shelters but with the annual tropical rains, and associated high humidity, pigments had become damp and flaked off. The paintings on vertical faces, where not renewed, seemed to Love, to have kept better than those in a horizontal position on overhangs.

When questioning men about a myth or painting, Love was referred to an elderly Aboriginal named *Kanaway* who was '. . . the recognised *Inaiiri* [literally, "great man", i.e. head], of the *Worrora*. The Kunmunya country . . . is Kanaway's own demesne. Is it a question concerning a rock or hill in the Kunmunya district? Kanaway knows all about it. Is it the meaning of a picture in this district? Kanaway knows all about it. Is it an old story of the mythical times? Kanaway knows all about these stories . . .'

For some years, he had been a pensioner at Kunmunya Mission and usually lived at the settlement where he received his food daily. But occasionally, *Kanaway* went 'walk-about', living in the bush for several weeks, then returning to resume his position as a pensioner.

Love records how *Kanaway* went for a 'tour' through his country during the last wet season of February-March, 1929. As one man told him '. . .he had gone to look at his country.' One week after his departure three new paintings, of the *kunjawrinya* (fresh-water tortoise), a *bulguja* (dugong), and a liver of stingray, *'ubunu'* were found on a rock overlooking the boat landing, at the place named *Ngaw-gaw*. These were on a rock-face where previously there were only faint signs of paintings that had been obliterated by the rain. Love continues: 'My two companions, young men, told me that Kanaway had made these new pictures. In public these two men

122

might have denied any knowledge of how these pictures got there, but to me, privately, they were ready to admit what was obvious to us all, that they had been freshly executed, and we all would have said without hesitation that Kanaway was the painter. I have not yet sufficient idiomatic command of the Worrora language to intimately discuss these things with Kanaway himself, as he is an old man, secretive, and not easy to approach through my stumbling Worrora tongue. I hope, in time, to learn much that will be of interest from himself. Meantime I have been pleased to have established the fact that the rock paintings, while some of them may be of vast antiquity (in sheltered positions), are mainly subject to renewal, or fresh execution, periodically, by Worrora men now living. This execution is done secretly, and the general mass of the tribe are told that the pictures are the work of no man's hand. Though an old man, with failing powers, Kanaway, as head of his people, still feels the urge to go out and ensure the food supply of his people by placing in the picture caves representations of the objects that need their pictures for their increase.'

In one painted cave, named *Nyimundum*, Love found an interesting and probably unique instance of an attempt to preserve designs from the rain. There were three paintings of *Warahninya* (the wedge-tailed eagle) in the cave. Over two of them was a semicircle of beeswax stuck on to the rock. This place was a *Woongguru* of one of the local Aborigines who was named *Nyimundum*, after the rock. Love asked him who had put beeswax over the eagle pictures. He thought his father might have been responsible but *Nyimundum's* father had been dead for some years and the beeswax lines had the appearance of being quite new. 'Evidently,' states Love, 'as Nyimundum had not visited this rock for about ten years before accompanying me, another man had put this protection on the rock. The painted rock-face is not exposed to the weather, but it slopes in such a way that rain falling on the top of the rock might run down and damage the pictures of the eagles. This rock, Nyimundum, supplies an instance of how the Worrora can hold two conflicting traditions without troubling to reconcile them. On the weathered under-surface of the rock are two pictures of Wonjuna. Both have the name Loongamunna. Loongamunna was a Wonjuna who came from the wind, walked about the country east of the Prince Regent River, then finally went to earth at this rock, where he left his picture, and where his *ingahnj* (spirit) evermore abides, ready to give children to men who may sleep and dream there.'

The age-old custom of re-touching was reported by Crawford (1968: 137-139) to have come to an end in the Kimberleys about twenty years ago. During an extensive investigation of sites, he found that only a very few paintings were being maintained; a restored painting was sometimes found but the majority were suffering from the ravages of time.

The customary practice of re-touching sacred paintings was obviously widespread. Arndt (1962: 163-170) was told that the famous Lightning Brothers on Delamere Station to the south-west of Katherine, were re-painted regularly for rain-making ceremonies. These paintings are believed to have been restored last in 1956.

In southern Australia, where rock paintings were abandoned 130 or so years ago, weathering has taken a large toll of the designs at most sites; there are very few situations where natural protection has preserved the pigments in their original condition.

Preservation of Wet Weather Shelter Art

The rigid adherence to designs laid down in the distant past was not a factor in all Aboriginal cave art. In the region under study and indeed over much of Arnhem Land, the painted decorations in shelters occupied mainly during the wet season were a record of daily life with a wide range of meanings and significance.

Galleries such as Obiri Rock, Deaf Adder Creek Valley, Inyalak Hill and Cannon Hill, are but four examples of extremely rich art sites. Hundreds of images in colourful ochres including fish, turtles, crocodiles, snakes, goannas, indeed all the food animals of the region, are superimposed one upon the other on the walls and ceilings of the caves. The extensive array of human figures illustrates much of the way of life of the people of the Alligator Rivers Region. The number of paintings is vastly more than found at sacred painting sites.

There are many instances of well protected painted walls and ceilings with superimpositions built up over centuries to provide 'history books' of the Arnhem Land people. Stylistic changes can be identified and also the introduction of new weapons such as the spear-thrower, boomerang and steel axe. It is interesting to note early paintings of figures using spears as javelins and later paintings portraying the

124

125

spear-thrower. The mass of information stored in this art is only beginning to be appreciated.

In traditional times there was no necessity for serious concern about preservation of paintings as it was custom to paint new designs in new positions or simply re-use areas of wall washed clean during the previous wet season. Constant painting in occupation shelters and re-touching of sacred designs ensured a continuing body of superb art. As is the case for sacred art it was only when the culture collapsed and paintings ceased to be an integral part of daily life that the full impact of weathering was noticed and there was a realisation by Aborigines that something was amiss. There has been a slow appreciation of the need to adopt general conservation procedures to preserve the art for future generations.

In a few remote areas Aborigines continue to follow some semblance of traditional life and indeed there is a strong movement to return to the 'bush' and follow the old ways. However, the pressures of change are very great and the need to bring rain, maintain natural food supplies, and perpetuate ancient beliefs, is no longer of prime importance; as a result few Aborigines paint in caves.

Many of the recent additions to the art of the Alligator Rivers Region are poor naturalistic representations of animals painted in plain white or yellow ochres. Some of these designs have been painted at the request of safari operators. The artists concerned lacked the spiritual motivation of traditional times and their work has little meaning in the context of traditional art.

There are exceptions to the general poor quality of recent art. Outstanding examples are at Nourlangie Rock and Nangaloar (Plate 37 bottom) where superb paintings of spirit figures and fish in X-ray style were executed in the 1960s with the same care and precision as used by the great artists of the past. The heritage of art in this region has been enriched by the addition of these drawings.

It is of interest that a new pigment, Reckitt's blue, was used in some of the Nourlangie designs. Spencer (1928: 831) noted that the Aborigines had a keen liking for blue, especially and unfortunately, he states, 'Reckitt's blue'. The use of this medium had not penetrated as far as Oenpelli in 1912 and Spencer hoped it would not be used in the traditional art of the area.

Available data shows quite clearly that rock art played an integral role in the daily life of the Aborigines in traditional times. It is unfortunate that the comparative isolation of the Alligator Rivers Region, due to the inhospitable nature of the vast wetlands and rugged escarpment country, limited the number of detailed studies made on rock art sites.

Disruption to Traditional Groups

The evidence gathered during the recent survey leads to the conclusion that few Aborigines maintain traditional associations with the art of the rock shelters. A major factor is the all but total disappearance of the *Kakadu* people who were the artists and custodians of much of the Alligator Rivers Region.

Since European contact and intrusion into the Alligator Rivers Region there has been considerable disruption to the different language groups. Peter Carroll has provided the following summary of the present situation:

Mangerr: Traditionally this is the language of the original group who lived at Oenpelli. They occupied the region around the coastal plain from Oenpelli to Arramunda where the new airstrip is located, and to the East Alligator River near Cahill's landing. There is a small group from this tribe still at Oenpelli.

Erre: A closely related language or dialect of *Mangerr*. This language was spoken by the inhabitants of the coastal plain area between Oenpelli and the River, particularly the Red Lily, the Crossing and Cannon Hill area. That is south and west of the *Mangerr* area. There are a few old women at Oenpelli who remember the language.

Uningangk: A closely related language or dialect of *Mangerr* and *Erre*. This language was spoken by the inhabitants of the coastal plain near where Tin Camp Creek meets the East Alligator River. That is south and east of the *Erre* area. There are a few old people at Oenpelli who remember the language.

Amurrak: A language spoken by people who lived north and west of the *Mangerr* area. Again the country is basically coastal plains along the East Alligator River. A few old people remember the language.

Iwaidja: Spoken by groups who lived north of Cooper's Creek towards Murgenella Creek.

Kakadju: An almost extinct language that is still remembered by a few old people. This group, mostly resident at Oenpelli, insist that the *Kakadju* country is the low country between the East and South Alligator Rivers. That is north and west of the present road between Mudginbarry and the East Alligator River crossing. The country along this road, particularly in the vicinity of Pan Continental Camp is said to be shared with the *Kundjeibmi* or *Djepmi* tribe.

Djepmi: This language is known and spoken by a number of people in the area and its traditional location was the stone country along the East Alligator River, upstream from Cahill's crossing and south and east from the crossing to Mudginbarry road.

Dangbon: A related language to *Gunwinggu* spoken by people who lived further into the stone country, south of *Gunwinggu* and east and south of *Djepmi*.

Gunwinggu: Currently this is the language spoken by the majority of the Aboriginal people at Oenpelli. Traditionally the *Gunwinggu* people lived east and south-east of Oenpelli. In the early days of the Mission, before the second World war, the majority of Aborigines contacted at Oenpelli were *Gunwinggu*. However, since the war there has been a considerable movement of Aborigines to Oenpelli from areas east and south-east of the *Gunwinggu* area. People from these areas are now resident at Oenpelli. The application of the word 'Gunwinggu' has been extended to cover people who traditionally would not have been called *Gunwinggu*. Older Aborigines at Oenpelli insist that even though these other groups can speak and understand *Gunwinggu* they are not true *Gunwinggu*. It seems that Europeans have applied the term to Aboriginal people who while a related group, are not strictly *Gunwinggu*.

Significance of Art

In common with the remainder of Aboriginal Australia, rock paintings are associated with only a small number of sites of special sacred significance.

Berndt (1970: 6) describes how 'in almost every part of Aboriginal Australia "tribal" territory is or was criss-crossed with a net-work of mythical tracks or "pathways" along which spirit beings are believed to have travelled . . . The actual sites themselves differ considerably. The most common are watering places or remarkably shaped rocks and other outstanding physiographic features, or caves and shelters, hills and gorges and so on. Some contain evidence of human artifice—for instance, rock and stone arrangements painting or incising; but many have no such marks to distinguish them from what can be regarded as ordinary non-mythical areas.' Carroll (1973: 1-23) in his survey of sites in the Nabarlek and associated regions lists sixty-four sites; rock paintings are associated with only six.

Although the traditional importance of much of the art has gone for all time, the rock paintings in the Alligator Rivers Region are a record of the history of the area and a source of identity to present generations of Aborigines.

CHAPTER 4

Antiquity of Rock Art

In common with many other aspects of Aboriginal culture, the precise origins of rock art are unknown. The advent of radiocarbon dating in 1950 enabled a time scale to be placed on stone tools, skeletal remains and other relics of the long Aboriginal occupation of Australia. However, perishable ochre paintings, such as those found in large numbers throughout the Alligator Rivers Region, have not survived in archaeological situations where dating methods can be applied. Evidence of age rests mainly on the recovery of fragments of ochre, many with worked facets, in widely separated occupation deposits. These provide convincing evidence of very great antiquity for paintings in many parts of Australia.

First discoveries

Aboriginal cave paintings have attracted the interest and curiosity of European explorers and settlers since the earliest contacts in the nineteenth century. Flinders (1814: 188-189) discovered paintings on Chasm Island while charting the Gulf of Carpentaria in January, 1803. He describes the art as '. . . rude drawings, made with charcoal and something like red paint upon the white ground of the rock. These drawings represented porpoises, turtle, kanguroos, and a human hand.'

Plate 37 (opposite) In recent years many paintings have been added to the galleries in the Alligator Rivers Region. *Top:* In December 1972 Bill Miyarki commemorated a visit to his country with wife and daughter by painting a small kangaroo in white pipe-clay next to an ancient red ochre figure of the same subject. The site is adjacent to the new access road to Koongarra. *Bottom:* A group of local fish at the Nangaloar gallery. *Left to Right:* Two barramundi, bream, freshwater garfish, sarratoga superimposed by a barrmundi and two catfish. These figures were painted in X-ray style in 1964.

Plate 38 Many factors contribute to the deterioration of rock paintings in the Alligator Rivers Region. *Top Left:* Water running down from the drip-line has removed much of the art at this site (Obiri Rock Region). *Top Right:* Some paintings are destroyed by flaking of the rock surface (Hawk Dreaming). *Bottom Left:* Water erosion, wasp nests and flaking have combined to destroy this section of a remote gallery (East Alligator River Crossing). *Bottom Right:* Hunter running with a spear in readiness to launch. Flaking of the white ochre will result in loss of this interesting painting (East Alligator River Crossing).

132

Further paintings were seen on Clack's Island during King's survey of the coastline of Cape York in 1821. Described as '. . . curious drawings . . .' they were '. . . executed upon a ground of red ochre, rubbed on the black schistus, and were delineated by dots of a white argillaceous earth, which had been worked up into a paste. They represented tolerable figures of sharks, porpoises, turtles, lizards (of which I saw several small ones among the rocks), trepang, star-fish, clubs, canoes, water-gourds, and some quadrupeds, which were probably intended to represent kangaroos and dogs. The figures besides being outlined by the dots, were decorated all over with the same pigment in dotted transverse belts. Tracing a gallery round to windward, it brought me to a commodious cave, or recess, overhung by a portion of the schistus, sufficiently large to shelter twenty natives, whose recent fire-places appear on the projecting area of the cave.

'Many turtles' heads were placed on the shelfs or niches of the excavation, amply demonstrative of the luxurious and profuse mode of life these outcasts of society had, at a period rather recently, followed. The roof and sides of this snug retreat were also entirely covered with the uncouth figures I have already described . . . this is the first specimen of Australian taste in the fine arts that we have detected in these voyages.' (King 1827: 26-27).

In 1838, during explorations in the Kimberley region of Western Australia, Grey found the large mouthless figures known to the Aborigines as 'Wandjinas'. He was one of the first to postulate on the antiquity of Aboriginal art: 'With regard to the age of these paintings', states Grey in his journal, (1841: 201-207) '. . . we had no clue whatever to guide us. It is certain that they may have been very ancient, for although the colours were composed of such perishable materials, they were all mixed with a resinous gum, insoluble in water, and no doubt, when thus prepared, they would be capable of resisting, for a long period, the usual atmospheric causes of decay. The painting which appeared to me to have been the longest executed was the one clothed in the long red dress, but I came to this conclusion solely from its state of decay and dilapidation, and these may possibly have misled me very much.'

Attempts to determine age through close examination of the condition of paintings, based as it is upon innumerable variables, has proved to be unsatisfactory. It is only since the recovery of ochre in dateable occupation deposits that less speculative determinations have been posssible.

As each part of the continent was opened up, the strange new art which had been an integral part of Aboriginal life for thousands of

133

years, attracted attention and the first of a long series of descriptive accounts appeared. Indeed, the records of Aboriginal paintings are as comprehensive and voluminous as those for any other aspect of their culture.

Stylistic variations

A range of different styles now has been identified in this art and linked with specific groups or localities. An obvious example, recognised by Spencer at Oenpelli in 1912, is the elaborate polychrome X-ray art of Arnhem Land with its detailed portrayal of skeleton and internal organs as well as external features (Spencer 1914: 443-449). The small monochrome *Mimi* figures, so common on the rock-faces of the Alligator Rivers Region, form another distinctive group. Equally significant are Grey's Wandjina paintings (Crawford 1968: 28-37), while another style has emerged from studies of cave art in western New South Wales where small human figures predominate. In central Australia, the Aboriginal of the desert portrayed his totemic ancestors in simple line, track and geometric motif (Strehlow 1964: 44-59). The final analysis of the large number of paintings recently discovered in Cape York by Trezise (1971: 7) should establish the existence of further styles in that area.

A more precise definition of art styles throughout the continent is certain to emerge as regional studies are pursued to greater depth (Edwards and Ucko 1973: 274-277).

Australia is unique insofar as it has been possible in some places to carry out intensive studies of rock art with the aid of Aborigines who regard it still as normal cultural expression (Davidson 1936: 108-120; Macintosh 1952: 256-274; Tindale 1959: 305-332; Arndt 1962: 298-320). In central Australia the Walbiri rituals associated with the *Ngama* and *Ruguri* cave painting sites play a significant role in what survives of tribal ceremonial life. Although, as discussed elsewhere in this report, in the traditional situation the degree of sanctity is known to have differed from group to group, the drawing or re-drawing of the figure of a mythical ancestor was usually intended to have some effect, direct or indirect, on their physical or spiritual environment.

Antiquity of Rock Engravings

Until the last decade of systematic archaeological excavation and positive dating of charcoal and other organic remains, speculation on the antiquity of Australian Aboriginal art has been limited mainly to the study of rock engravings. The permanence of the designs cut deeply into the surfaces of rocks has been the only direct access to the artistic expression of long past generations.

The study of rock engravings began in much the same way as that of paintings; the existence of engravings being noted by early explorers, navigators and settlers.

Among the first to refer to Aboriginal engraved designs was Captain Arthur Phillip, the first Governor of New South Wales, who, within three months of setting foot in Australia in January, 1788, located an extensive series of large outline engravings in the Sydney district. 'The natives of New South Wales', said a chronologer of the day, 'though so rude and uncivilized a state as not even to have made an attempt towards clothing themselves, notwithstanding that at times they evidently suffer from the cold and wet, are not without notions of sculpture. In all these excursions of Governor Phillip, and in the neighbourhood of Botany Bay and Port Jackson, the figures of animals, of shields, and weapons, and even of men, have been seen carved upon the rocks, roughly indeed, but sufficiently well to ascertain very fully what was the object intended. Fish were often represented, and in one place the form of a large lizard was sketched out with tolerable accuracy. On the top of one of the hills, the figure of a man in the attitude usually assumed by them when they begin to dance, was executed in a still superior style. That the arts of imitation and amusement should thus in any degree precede those of necessity, seems an exception to the rules laid down by theory for the progress of invention. But perhaps it may better be considered as a proof that the climate is never so severe as to make the provision of covering or shelter a matter of absolute necessity. Had these men been exposed to a colder atmosphere, they would doubtless have had clothes and houses, before they attempted to become sculptors.' (Stockton 1789: 106-107).

In north-west Australia, Stokes (1846 Vol. 2: 170-172) reported human figures, animals, birds, weapons and implements engraved on rock surfaces. 'This group of islands is so connected with the mainland by extensive sand-banks, that at low water it is possible to walk across to them; and of this facility the natives no doubt avail themselves to procure turtles. It appears indeed to be only on such occasions that they can visit the Forestier Group, as we saw no traces of rafts on this portion of the coast. Depuch Island would seem to be their favourite resort; and we found several of their huts still standing. They were constructed of boughs and twigs fixed in the ground, and joined overhead in a circular shape. Over this was thrown a loose matting of twisted grass. The natives are doubtless attracted to the place partly by the reservoirs of water they find among the rocks after rain, partly that they may enjoy the pleasure of delineating the various objects that attract their attention, on the smooth surface of the rocks. This they do by removing the hard red outer coating, and baring to view the natural colour of the greenstone, according to the outline they have traced. Much ability is displayed in many of these representations, the subjects of which could be discovered at a glance. The number of specimens was immense, so that the natives must have been in the habit of amusing themselves in this innocent manner for a long period of time. I could not help reflecting, as I examined with interest the various objects represented—the human figures, the animals, the birds, the weapons, the domestic implements, the scenes of savage life—on the curious frame of mind that could induce these uncultivated people to repair, perhaps at stated seasons of the year, to this lonely picture gallery, surrounded by the ocean-waves, to admire and add to the productions of their forefathers. No doubt they expended on their works of art as much patience and labour and enthusiasm as ever was exhibited by a Raphael or a Michael Angelo in adorning the walls of St. Peter or the Vatican; and perhaps the admiration and applause of their fellow-countrymen imparted as much pleasure to their minds as the patronage of popes and princes, and the laudation of the civilized world, to the great masters of Italy.'

Gradually, other sites were located in widely separated parts of the continent, the initial finds proving to be but a small extension of a large mainland series.

Prehistoric rock engravings, neither so obvious nor so immediately attractive as the colourful paintings, were often overlooked by early investigators and their study has been slow to develop. It is only in the last decade that the great number and wide distribution of engravings has begun to be realised (Mountford 1960: 145-147; Edwards 1968: 665-666).

Distribution of Rock Engravings

Although a pattern of regional distribution of rock engraving styles is emerging, this is not so clearly developed as that claimed for paintings. In fact it is becoming increasingly apparent that there is a number of constant features common to many sites in widely separated areas of the continent. These features are—close proximity of engravings to regular sources of water, advanced weathering and surface patination and consistent relative frequencies of designs.

It is of interest that dense concentrations of stone tools are rarely associated with engraving sites, although it is true, for example in the Woomera area of South Australia, that there are engravings at

Eucolo Creek (Hall *et al.* 1951: 375-380) not far distant from some of the densest concentrations of artifacts in Australia. This is an exceptional situation as normally there is only a sparse scatter of implements, with perhaps a few types represented and then in small numbers.

It may be significant that, at an increasing number of engraved sites, large trimmed core implements are being found. These are identical in type to the so-called 'Kartan' industry first identified from sites on Kangaroo Island, on the Adelaide Plains and elsewhere (Cooper 1943: 343-369). There are even some situations where large collections of these crude tools have been found to the exclusion of other more sophisticated industries. During examination of engraving sites in central Australia many of these same implements were found, thus extending their known distribution far beyond anything previously recorded.

As there is some evidence to suggest great antiquity for large trimmed core industries, the progressively emerging association of these tools with engravings presents an aspect worthy of further study. They are common on Kangaroo Island, unoccupied at the time of its discovery by Flinders in March, 1802 (Cooper 1960: 481). It has been shown in studies of the Lake Mungo sites in western New South Wales that core industries have existed in Australia for over 30 000 years.

It is interesting to note that despite a close search, no tools have been found which can be identified as having been made specifically for engraving designs on rock surfaces (Edwards 1971: 359). As the individual 'peck' marks that go to make up an engraved design differ considerably in size and shape in each instance, it is highly probable that the rock engravers did not develop a specialised tool for engraving.

Evidence of Antiquity

A consistent feature of most engraving sites is the advanced weathering and disintegration of engraved rock surfaces. However, surface weathering can indicate only that some sites are old while others are of more recent origin. There are too many variables to admit positive dating by this means at the present time (Edwards 1971: 260-261).

The identification of a few engravings of outsized kangaroo, wombat and bird tracks as those of extinct animals seems to some to be speculative, yet as dates for man and his engraved art go back in time, so do dates for extinct animals come forward.

Such engravings may simply be those of giant mythical creatures of the Aboriginal Dreamtime, present only in the minds of the people who made them. Alternatively, the increasing evidence of great antiquity for engravings admits the possibility of a contemporaneous existence for the rock engraving people and giant animals. If this is shown to be correct, it would not be surprising to find engraved tracks of extinct creatures in prehistoric Australian art.

It may be significant that the tracks of the dingo are rarely found among the many thousands of animal tracks at widely distributed sites. When they do occur, their earliest presence is so far not attested before about 7 000 years ago; its all but total absence from this presumed ancient art form may be more than coincidence (Campbell, *et al.* 1966: 10).

Despite their apparent sophistication, profile engravings, which are found at sites in most areas where engravings occur, are not of recent origin, because the age indicators of advanced weathering and heavy patination also are constant. It is only at sites on the west Australian coast (Wright 1968: 1-78; McCarthy 1962: 1-73) that a later proliferation of the human figure has occured. That this rich array of animated and sometimes grotesque human figures is a later development is indicated by the 'freshness' of the engravings and their corresponding lack of patination.

Engravings recovered in archaeological excavations

The first indication of real antiquity for rock engravings came in 1929, with the discovery of abraded grooves on the back wall of the Devon Downs rock shelter, on the lower River Murray in South Australia, at a depth of between three and four metres below ground surface. Hale and Tindale (1930: 208-210) linked the Devon Downs engravings with so-called 'Pirrian-Mudukian' layers dated at 3 500 to 2 500 years ago: outline engravings were associated with the late 'Mudukian' and early 'Murundian' of 2 500 to 1 500 years ago and linear designs with the late 'Murundian' from 1 500 years ago to the present time.

McCarthy (1962: 1-73) when considering the age of the engravings at Port Hedland, found little positive evidence to indicate their antiquity. The fact that three phases of engraving had been passed through suggested that a considerable period of time had elapsed since they were made. By relating the evidence and radiocarbon datings from Devon Downs, McCarthy considers that rock engravings at Port Hedland have been carried on for some 3 000 years and probably much longer.

In addition, concerning engravings at Depuch Island, McCarthy (1961: 145) states '. . . the antiquity of rock engravings of Depuch Island covers a considerable period of time, probably several thousands of years. Most of the figures in the first outline naturalistic period are in a faded condition, as are, however, many of the later intaglios. On the other hand, many of the figures in the second or design period and a large number of the intaglios are perfectly preserved.' McCarthy felt that state of preservation was an unreliable guide to the age of engravings.

Davidson (1952: 101) was of the opinion that the historic age of engravings in north-west Australia could not be determined as there was no chronological base on which to calculate estimates. Attempts to obtain precise dates were frustrated by lack of situations where positive dating could be applied.

Positive dating for engravings

The rather blurred image of an ancient prehistoric art in Australia came sharply into focus in 1966, when conclusive datings were obtained for engraved material found in an excavation undertaken by Mulvaney on Willeroo Station, 160 kilometres south-west of Katherine in the Northern Territory. The walls of the sandstone outcrop in which the site is located are completely covered with engravings and paintings. The weathered and patinated appearance of many engravings suggest great antiquity, but others, including one of a sailing ship, are obviously of recent origin. The excavation trench was sited adjacent to a heavily engraved part of the wall in the hope that the engravings and paintings would continue below ground level where they could be assigned minimum ages by dating charcoal in the overlying levels. Unfortunately, the back wall of the shelter was smooth and bare except for one small group of abraded grooves.

However, as mentioned previously, detached rock fragments bearing emu and kangaroo tracks and abraded grooves, were excavated later in the main body of the trench and dated to 7 000 years ago. This gives support to the idea of considerable antiquity for other

140

rock engravings, and it is hoped that situations will be found where precise datings can be obtained for a wider range of designs and techniques.

Discovery of earliest art

At Koonalda on the Nullarbor Plain, detailed study of simple wall engravings on an inner passage of the deep limestone cave produced evidence for even greater antiquity of Australian rock art (Edwards and Maynard 1967: 11-17; Gallus 1968: 43-49). Charcoal collected between boulders near dense concentrations of markings has been dated to about 20 000 years ago. As the area is in total darkness, this charcoal is thought to have come from crude torches used by prehistoric man who visited the cave to mine flint. There are two main types of markings: hand smears made by running fingers over areas of the wall which are soft and talc-like, and incised lines abraded or scratched into the harder surfaces. It is interesting that the abraded grooves are similar to those found in the Ingaladdi excavation and at other widely distributed sites (Edwards 1965: 17-18).

It seems unlikely that any direct association between engravings and charcoal will be firmly established at Koonalda. However, their antiquity is supported by the existence of large areas of engravings under fifteen metres of rock-falls, some of which must date to 20 000 years ago. Although the constant environmental conditions in the cave have reduced the extent of weathering, its effects may be clearly seen. The edges of all the finger markings on the walls, except those few known to be of recent origin, are smooth. At the same time, scrape marks caused by the ancient fall of boulders now wedged below massive rock-falls still retain a fresh appearance.

Koonalda offers unique evidence for Aboriginal art in Australia. Similar markings have been found on the walls of a number of European caves including Altimira. These are believed by Breuil and Berger-Kirchner (1961: 26) to be the earliest signs of man's artistic endeavours in the Upper Palaeolithic, some 30 000 years ago. Possibly the simple wall markings at Koonalda are an isolated and extensive example of the earliest stage of artistic evolution in Australia which is consistent with the long-held view that abraded grooves constitute the first phase of Aboriginal rock art (McCarthy 1964: 33).

Some special significance may be attached to the engravings recorded in Tasmania. The most extensive site is at Mt Cameron West, on the north-west coast, where deeply engraved circles and simple arrangements of lines are closely massed on a large outcrop of aeolianite on the beach, a little above high tide mark. Such a situation is unusual for Australian rock engravings.

The Tasmanian engravings have many mainland parallels, especially in south and central Australia. Since the techniques and designs used are identical, the implication is that the art must date back to a pre-Bass Strait period of some 12 000 years ago. It might be inferred from the very extensive distribution that many engravings pre-date the time when separate cultural entities had developed.

It may be significant that few rock engraving sites have been found in the Alligator Rivers Region. At this stage in its examination, the area appears not to have been frequented regularly by the rock engraving people who left their markings over a wide area of the continent.

Ochres associated with dateable deposits

The impermanence of ochre paintings which demand continual retouching for preservation, has made assessments of their antiquity difficult. However, the age of Aboriginal rock art is no longer confined to analysis of engravings. As Stanner (1960: 22) suggests, it is possible to match ochres from particular paintings with used ochres taken from cave and floor deposits which can be dated from organic substances found in situations associated with them.

The investigations carried out in 1947 at Tandandjal Cave, south-west Arnhem Land, by Macintosh (1951: 178-213) were among the first to produce evidence of an association between paintings and ochre fragments found in archaeological excavations of cave deposits. Red and white ochres were found in the floor debris. The size of the fragments ranged from one centimetre across up to large lumps fifteen centimetres in diameter. The distribution of colour '. . . in the trench . . .', states Macintosh, '. . . accords quite well with the paintings on the outer and inner galleries.'

Although no age was postulated for these discoveries, an association between art and excavated ochres was established and provided a pointer for later studies.

The most important evidence of age for cave paintings and, indeed an antiquity comparable to that attributed to prehistoric engravings, came from Mulvaney's excavations at Kenniff Cave on Mt Moffatt Station in southern Queensland.

Although the walls of the caves were richly decorated no trace of art was found on the portions uncovered by excavations carried out from 1960 to 1964. Ochre-clay, weathered basalt, and ferruginous sandstone fragments were present in all layers at the two sites investigated. A number of the ochre fragments found had been smoothed and scratched with rubbing. As many of the scratches are longitudinal grooves, Mulvaney inferred that they were rubbed to-

142

and-fro, rather than with a circular motion. One of the small basalt pieces recovered during the excavation had been smoothed on nine distinct facets, indicating prolonged use.

The presence of ochres in the Kenniff Cave deposits is an indication that even the Pleistocene colonists of Australia possessed some aesthetic sense, whether they painted themselves, their implements or on cave walls.

As dates in the order of 19 000 can be attributed to the earliest finds, it is reasonable to suppose that the artists brought some pigments to Kenniff Cave before the artists of Lascaux and Altimara painted their masterpieces (Mulvaney 1965: 201).

Archaeological excavations undertaken by McCarthy while the 1948 Arnhem Land Expedition was camped at Oenpelli, provided further examples of excavated ochre associated with rock paintings. McCarthy and Setzler (1960: Vol. 2: 218-219) report: 'At Oenpelli there appears to be a direct connection between the occupational deposits in the floors of the rock shelters and the paintings on their walls and ceilings. Most of the rock shelters excavated here contain paintings or were adjacent to one or other of the extensive art galleries. These paintings cover a wide range of Australian techniques and styles, such as outline drawings, silhouettes, linear figures, including the *Mimi* art, polychromes, including the X-ray type; at Inagurdurwil there are also hand stencils. On the basis of present evidence, the mixture of stone implement traits in the deposits seems to indicate that all of these techniques of painting were practised by the natives who used the sites for habitation and for ritual drawing purposes. A study of the super-imposing of the paintings in this area indicates that a succession of techniques may exist, but distinct cultural horizons could neither be determined by stratification in the deposits, nor linked with these various painting techniques or periods. The numerous examples of used pieces of red, yellow and white pigments found in the deposits, however, is convincing evidence that the people who made and used the implements associated with them are also responsible for the paintings.

'It should also be mentioned that outline, silhouettes and polychrome paintings are represented further south in the Wardaman caves and also at Tandandjal with stencils.

'There is a great variety of shapes among the pieces of pigment, including rectangular, triangular and round, and pieces are either flat, wedge-like, pyramidal, or irregular in form. Most of the haematite, is greyish-black in colour, but where it has decomposed it is from pink to red. There are from one to nine rubbed faces on the pieces, the pyramidal ones being rubbed on all surfaces, including the bottom, and there are often several facets on the one surface. Most of the floors are rocky and any debris present consists of recently discarded pandanus seeds and a few shells. This made it impossible to link the paintings and their development with the existing stone culture. The colour shades vary considerably in the reds and yellows.'

A further correlation between paintings and ochre found in deposits, was established by Macintosh at a rock shelter complex on the south-eastern slopes of Mt Manning some one hundred kilometres north of Sydney.

There are two shelters in the complex (south and north) both of which contain Aboriginal paintings. Macintosh (1965: 85-101) states, 'The paintings are divisible into two art traditions; the earlier is represented by a ritual group of six large dark red ochre paintings in the Southern Shelter; the more recent by a sequence of light red ochre, charcoal and white paintings in the Northern Shelter.

'Total excavation of the floor deposit in the Northern Shelter revealed one patch of light red ochre, a meagre stone assemblage of two Bondi points, one bifaced adze blade with gum adherent, two microlithic cores, 68 waste flakes and 73 fragments of bone, teeth, shell. This indicates that the North Shelter was not a workshop nor a feeding place; but the fire blackened roof and heavily charcoalised floor deposit indicate that occupancy was frequent. Other caves in the vicinity are more suitable for shelter from the elements, yet are sterile. The only explanation for the occupancy of the Northern Shelter would therefore seem to be related to the paintings.

'Excavation of the undisturbed platform deposit at the northern extremity of the Southern Shelter revealed only ochre and charcoal. The actual Southern Shelter itself contains the impressive ritualistic paintings . . . otherwise there is no evidence whatever of any intrusion.

'The paintings of the Northern Shelter complex . . . show a colour sequence of earliest red outline, followed by red infilled, then charcoal, and latest white. The red paintings have the same chroma, hue and value as the superficial ochre layer (in the excavation) which is immediately below a charcoal layer radiocarbon dated as A.D. 1806 and A.D. 1830. Hence the Northern Shelter paintings apparently range in age from approximately A.D. 1750 to A.D. 1830. These paintings appear to be secular, profane rather than sacred, confined to depicting the local fauna and the hunting of it for food. Medium, style and technique seem to have been convention bound and this art-school is represented also in a cave 9.3 miles [15 km] to the south-east.

'The ritual group . . . in the Southern Shelter are quite different

144

in style, technique and medium and clearly belong to a different art tradition and embody a different philosophy from the Northern Series. Their chroma, hue and value matches the deep stratum of ochre in the excavation, which provided also an ochre nodule; three of its surfaces are flattened by grinding and it gives the same Munsel reading as the ochre deposit and the paintings. Charcoal from a closed fire hearth immediately beneath it was radiocarbon dated at A.D. 1369, so that the paintings apparently were made at approximately A.D. 1400.

'There is an hiatus of some 350 years between the Southern Shelter and Northern Shelter series. Five strata of charcoal occur in the floor deposit during this interval of time. It seems unlikely that the ritual group was subject to re-touching. Altered or blurred margins might be anticipated if such had been the case, and additional strata of pigment would have been expected in the excavation . . . the Southern Shelter is exclusively the province of the ritual group. Not so much as the presence of a single hand stencil intrudes upon them. It would seem that an earlier aura of sanctity was respected throughout the subsequent painting periods. They probably continued to be regarded as sacrosanct, even though their tradition and interpretation may have become archaic in terms of the more mundane expressions of the later series of paintings.' (Macintosh 1965: 97-8.)

Recent dating of ochres

In recent years there has been a spate of systematic excavations which has led to further correlation between pieces of ochre from dated levels and rock art on associated cave walls. In Cape York where dense concentrations of paintings have been recorded, Wright (1971: 139) reports 'Ground ochre of various shades is profusely distributed from top to bottom of the deposit and the age of the paintings present on the walls cannot therefore be postulated from the occurrence of ochres. It is worth noting, however, that the shallow deposits of nearby painted shelters always yield the recent [stone tool] industry . . .

'There are numerous paintings on the walls and ceilings of the excavated cave, however, they do not survive below the floor surface, mainly because of termite damage. At two metres, the lowest position in the sequence from which charcoal was collected, a date of 6 870± 150 BP was obtained; earlier dates can be expected as the deposit continues to four metres.'

At Stanner's Yarar Rock Shelter near Port Keats, ochre was an outstanding component of the deposit, weighing a total of 183 kilograms and comprising some 20 000 pieces. Stanner found that the greatest concentration occurred towards the centre of the shelter underneath the thickest cluster of paintings. A later detailed study was made by Flood (1970: 22-52) of all the ochre from one square in which ochre was well represented in each of five levels. All pieces were counted except those of less than half a centimetre square, yielding a total of 1 439 pieces. A closer study of 978 lumps which showed signs of use revealed an average weight of twenty grammes. Their size varied from six centimetres to less than half a centimetre, but more than half the pieces, used and unused, were in the one to two centimetres range. Most of the used pieces were rounded to a pebble-like shape, but one was of a conical form with highly polished round and octagonal sides. It was harder than the other ochre and darker in colour.

A colour analysis was carried out by Flood on the 978 used pieces in the hope that there might be changes in the predominant colour of ochre according to level, which could be correlated with periods of paintings on the rock walls of this and perhaps other shelters. 'Five basic colours were found to occur, a red-orange, a dark brown (ranging from near black to a rich chocolate colour), a light brown, white and yellow. Disappointingly, there seemed no significant change in the colour of the ochre pieces from the upper to lower levels. Red-orange predominated throughout, followed by dark and light brown, with just a little white and yellow.'

There were some discrepancies in the dating of the deposit, however, the maximum age was estimated to be only about 3 000 years.

There are many superimposed paintings on the walls of the shelter. The majority are described as highly abstracted types of linear or geometric styles, with very few human figures and some stencilled handprints. Flood (1970: 29) considers '. . . the density and complexity of the Yarar art may indicate a long period of occupation despite reasonably late dates . . .' It is significant also that this site was a wet weather shelter; the paintings may have been executed during periods of comparative immobility.

Similar evidence was found in central Australia by Gould (1968: 3) whose excavations at Puntutjarpa in the Warburton Range area of Western Australia led to the recovery of red ochre in deposits dated to about 7 000 years ago.

Applying an ethnographic analogy, Gould (1968: 174) states: 'Red ochre figures prominently in the ceremonial life of the Ngatatjara, and evidently it has been important throughout the history of human habitation at this site. Lumps of red ochre, all showing definite striations from grinding wear, occur sporadically between depths of six and forty eight inches [15.24 cm and 121 cm]. The Ngatatjara carry lumps of red ochre with them, often in emu-feather bundles, as they move from place to place. These lumps show the same kind of wear as the archaeological specimens and were probably used in much the same way as they are today (i.e. for ritual body-painting, rock-painting, and for coating sacred objects and other artifacts). It is not known where the ochre found at the site was quarried.'

Ochres dating back over 5 000 years were reported from two art sites in the Graman district of New South Wales by McBryde (1968: 81). In the deposits at both sites fragments of red pigment were recovered from all levels, some of them bearing marks of rubbing on stone, while from one of the trenches, at a site containing concentrations of engravings, came a grinding stone with clear traces of red pigment on its grinding surface.

'However, all this evidence for the use and preparation of red paints could well be associated with the decoration of wooden artifacts, or of the bodies of the inhabitants for ceremonial occasions rather than with rock paintings', states McBryde, 'The pigments could all be obtained locally, both the red, and the yellow which is found in the deposits, but not represented in the rock paintings. It is tempting to associate the paintings at [one site] with the period of occupation, especially as these paintings, in spite of their protected position, are faded with age, and in several places are cut by a honeycomb weathering of the sandstone. This must give them an antiquity of at least several centuries.' (McBryde 1968: 90).

Ochre has been found also in caves not used for painting. 'White Kangaroo' cave on Arguluk Hill near Oenpelli is a good example. McCarthy and Setzler (1960: 270) state that '. . . some 666 objects were recovered of which 452 were pigment stones. Of these 436 are red ochre or haematite; three yellow ochre; seven pink, consisting of sandstone and shale with rubbed surfaces; and six white pigments from shale and micaceous shale.

'It seems somewhat unusual that we should find 557 rubbed pieces of various pigments in these two caves on Arguluk, while most of the cave paintings appear on [nearby] Gunbalanja. They were apparently used on Arguluk to decorate perishable objects, such as spears, spear-throwers, baskets, ceremonial objects, as well as the bones of the dead, and the bodies of dancers and those participating in ceremonies. Only the few paintings on the ceiling and back wall of this cave are at all obvious.'

There is no doubt that ochre had a wide range of uses. Evidence of association with mortuary rites was found at Kow Swamp in northern Victoria, one of the major Australian burial sites. Some excavated remains had been coated with red ochre; other pieces were found

148

in graves together with shell and stone artifacts. Dates ranging back over 13 000 years have been obtained for these important finds (Thorne pers. comm.). Even in Tasmania, where there are few records of paintings, Jones (pers. comm.) found ochre throughout the 8 000 year old Rocky Cape deposits. Again at Cloggs Cave, Buchanin, in Victoria, Flood (pers. comm.) found ochre fragments in deposits dated to nearly 18 000 years, while in the Ord River District of Western Australia, Dortch (pers. comm.) has found new evidence of the use of ochre since 18 000 years ago.

Some of the most recent finds have been made in the Alligator Rivers Region where White (1967: 136) reports an association between ochre and rock art dating back to 22 000 years and Allen and Kamminga (1973: 95) report the 'Lindner' site in Deaf Adder Creek Valley as having ochre at a level dated at 19 960 ± 280 BP.

Of particular significance is the evidence from Lake Mungo in western New South Wales where Mulvaney (pers. comm.) has recovered from excavations, ochres dated to at least 30 000 years ago.

Ancient cultural traits as time markers

It has been possible to gain some indication of the relative age of paintings by a close study of the designs themselves. This is particularly relevant to the Alligator Rivers Region where different cultural traits were portrayed by the Aboriginal artists.

The introduction of the spear-thrower is a good example. Davidson (1936: 445) believes the spear-thrower to be one of the most important inventions in human history. Used by Upper Palaeolithic hunters in Europe 20 000 years ago, this device offers a double advantage to those who use spears for it not only increases the leverage of the arm, thereby permitting the attainment of a more distant range, but it also concentrates the entire force of delivery behind the butt of the spear to allow greater accuracy.

The absence of the spear-thrower in Tasmania, where Aborigines had been isolated culturally for some 12 000 years, is evidence that the earliest Australians lacked spear-throwers when they first entered the continent.

149

Portrayal of hunters in Alligator Rivers Region art using spears as javelins and/or lances, and other paintings showing spear-throwers in use, may provide a reliable basis for comparative analysis of the different styles and place them in a time sequence.

Spears themselves are shown in great detail with a range of heads, including plain, barbed, multi-pronged and stone. The same analogy can be used for boomerangs which did not find their way to Tasmania during the period when it was attached to the mainland.

Brandl (1973: 171-178) has used these criteria in establishing art styles in western and central Arnhem Land. He has identified also paintings of the Tasmanian Tiger associated with *Mimi* art while dogs and dingoes occur in X-ray art and other recent styles. It can be assumed that Tasmanian Tigers were not painted after they became extinct on the mainland many thousands of years ago.

The rather subjective evidence from the art itself supports the general proposition that ochre painting has been an important and continuous tradition in the Alligator Rivers Region for many thousands of years, indeed there is every reason to believe that painting came to Australia with the first arrivals over 30 000 years ago. Its perishability has meant certain destruction when in exposed situations. However, preservation of ochres in dateable stratified deposits is of great significance, particularly when there is a correlation with art on the walls of the rock shelters concerned.

In the Alligator Rivers Region, the survey undertaken as part of the Environmental Fact Finding Study, has shown the region to be highly significant as it contains art sites of undoubted antiquity. Scientific study of such sites may well produce irrefutable evidence to show that Australian rock paintings are among the oldest in the world.

CHAPTER 5

Factors Contributing to Deterioration
of Paintings

In the Alligator Rivers Region where summer rains amount to upwards of 1 400 millimetres (55 in.), it is inevitable that the natural forces of weathering are very great. Indeed the cave art of the area is being subjected to a relentless onslaught by a wide range of destructive forces.

The state of preservation of paintings ranges from very poor to almost perfect. Paintings in well protected rock overhangs have a favourable advantage over those exposed to weathering. Some designs are barely discernible on rock surfaces, while others appear to have survived in their original condition. There is an enormous range of variables. No two shelters are alike; each site has its own characteristics and must be taken as an individual unit and corrective measures considered in accordance with the factors involved.

The causes of deterioration are many and varied: water washes over some painted surfaces in most galleries while in others mould grows on walls and ceilings. Termites build channels over many paintings, wasps construct mud nests on ancient designs and animals rub against them. In some shelters environmental conditions are such that plants take root in crevices and gradually prise rocks apart; in many instances roots grow over the paintings themselves. Wind-borne sand abrades some rocks and dust clings to surfaces—obliterating designs. Despite the remoteness of the region there are instances where vandals have scrawled names across paintings. All these factors contribute to the continual deterioration of the large concentration of rock art in the Alligator Rivers Region.

As the survival of ochre paintings is dependent upon innumerable variables it is difficult to make general comparisons with sites elsewhere. Cave art in other parts of tropical Australia (Arnhem Land, the Kimberleys and Cape York) is affected by similar conditions, while in

151

central Australia water erosion and moulds are not so troublesome but wind erosion, fretting and exfoliation create greater havoc. In the south, where vandalism is rife, the overall dangers are also very great. It can be said as a statement of fact that the rock art of Australia is in grave danger of all but total destruction unless adequate conservation and protective measures are taken.

Preservation of Paintings in Other Regions

Mountford (1965: 181-182) found obvious indications of the deleterious effects of weathering upon cave art at Ayers Rock in central Australia. Paintings in one shallow cave facing the open plain only a few metres south of *Mutitjilda* rock shelter, were clear and fresh when first seen in 1935. Many of the designs had practically disappeared by 1959. Two other paintings had completely weathered away in the same period. By contrast, a line of colourful human figures, reptiles and abstract designs in a protected shelter, had suffered little damage.

In the Kimberleys, Crawford (1968: 81) notes numerous faded and eroded figures; indeed the discovery of a distinct painting was said to be a rare event. 'The sun has faded them and the rain eroded them. Occasionally even the rock surface on which the paintings have been made has fretted, leaving only sections of the original features', recorded Crawford.

Comparisons made by Trezise and Wright (1966: 320-324) of records of cave art on Dunk Island, north Queensland, suggest that there were no gross changes in the condition of paintings in a granite rock shelter over a period of some sixty years. The extreme dryness of the shelter ensured the protection of the art despite the high rainfall and humidity of the island.

Any assessment of the relative importance of sites in the Alligator Rivers Region must take into account the state of preservation of each site and its capability of being preserved and protected in the future.

Water Erosion

During the wet season immense torrents of water run over the rocks forming the Arnhem Land escarpment and its outliers. Much of it finds its way on to areas of rock-face painted with innumerable ochre designs. The total and/or partial removal of paintings by water erosion is a predominant factor of destruction, accounting for something in the order of seventy per cent of all damage.

The amount of art affected in each situation varies and is dependent upon the location and shape of the shelter. The area of catchment also has a direct influence on the quantity of water which runs, splashes, and/or drips on to painted surfaces. The problem is aggravated when the painted gallery is at the base of the escarpment or a large residual, as in such situations huge volumes of water cascade over the site during the peak of the wet season.

The intensity of flow and direction of the wind also are contributing factors and have a direct relationship to the area and position of washed surfaces. These factors are extremely variable, e.g. surfaces in the path of the flow will be washed by water every time it rains; others may be affected only after intensive rain for a given period, with a wind blowing from a particular direction. It is unpredictable freak conditions that were, and indeed still are, the most destructive.

Aboriginal artists avoided regular water channels for painting as the rocks were stained black, often covered with lichen and generally unsuitable. However, as the position of the drainage was at no time static it must often have been difficult to predict where water would flow. The channels themselves would erode, particularly where rocks were soft. Water-borne sand can cut quite rapidly into rocks changing the direction of flow, which results in certain damage to paintings that were previously sheltered.

Each shelter and overhang has a natural drip-line at which point the water pouring over the outer surfaces drops to the ground. Although these water-lines can be quite precise, they do vary in accordance with the intensity of flow. There are many instances where the angle of the rock is such that the water fails to drip to the ground, but runs back over the ceiling causing havoc to paintings. One of many extreme examples was found in a cave high on the hillside on the Nourlangie-Mt Brockman massif. Water running back from the drip-line has erased a large and important group of painted designs (Plate 26 bottom).

Seepage can also be a continuing problem. Water often filters through crevices and fractures, finding its way to the back walls or ceilings of shelters. Paintings well away from the weather can be seriously affected. Even during the winter dry season, water from the plateau continues to find its way, under pressure, into shelters, sometimes providing a permanent supply of useful spring water.

The porosity of rock is yet another variable affecting the life of paintings. Designs made on hard quartzite rocks could be washed away in a single shower. When paint was applied to more porous surfaces it often became impregnated into the rock making removal difficult. There are examples at Cannon Hill and at many other sites, where red ochre designs, in particular *Mimi* figures, have become an integral component of the rock. Relatively frequent wetting seems to have had little affect upon their condition. Such designs, when first painted, may have been vulnerable to weathering and the surface pigments washed away but a permanent red stain has been left in the rock surface.

There is every prospect of survival for some centuries for these examples of Aboriginal art.

There are instances also where a thin sinter deposit has formed by percolation of water through the rock. This constitutes a binding element similar to calcium hydrate. Sometimes this forms 'glassy' protective films over art works making them indestructible. However such films tend to obscure details of the designs.

It is impossible to estimate the toll already taken by water erosion. Conservators agree that water is the worst single factor in the weathering of rock art sites (Walston 1972: 223). In the case of shelters exposed to the full impact of erosion, upwards of ninety per cent of the art has been washed away, while damage to paintings in shelters well protected from the weather is usually confined to those near the exposed edges and along the drip-line, with the main body of art preserved intact.

There are innumerable examples of extreme water damage in the Alligator Rivers Region, indeed, few sites have escaped damage from this causation. The main painted rock-faces at sites in Tin Camp Creek Valley (Plate 39 top) are typical of many shelters. Here a vast array of significant paintings has been washed away causing ruination to once important galleries of ancient art.

However many the variables, the combined effect of water erosion on rock art is quite enormous. Ideally, water should be totally excluded. In the case of rock shelters, dampcoursing and roofing of entire structures would be a monumental undertaking, but it would be possible to experiment on a smaller scale. Total exclusion of water from painted surfaces would certainly give any preservation techniques a better chance of success (Walston 1972: 223).

Installation of artificial drains to divert water from affected surfaces would be a first step in the preservation of the large number of paintings threatened by continual exposure to water erosion.

Moulds

Many painted designs have been destroyed by mould and lichen growth during the intense humidity of the northern wet season.

Moulds and lichens require special environmental conditions to spawn and multiply. Fortunately, the Aborigines made almost exclusive use of rock shelters and overhangs. The preference for large, canopy-type rock shelters, minimises the instances of mould damage. The Aborigines avoided many problems by shunning deep, dark, damp caverns, that were available in some parts of the escarpment. However, as ideal sites were not always conveniently placed, some less suitable caves were occupied.

It is interesting to note that in some instances the Aborigines were attracted into deep caves. The best example is at Koonalda on the Nullarbor Plain, where extensive areas of hand markings and abraded grooves have been found on cave walls in total darkness (Edwards and Maynard 1968: 15). A study of this art and radiocarbon dating of associated charred wood, believed to be the remains of torches used to light the deep underground chambers, dates it to around 20 000 years ago. This is the earliest occurrence of rock art outside of Palaeolithic Europe.

Lichen growth has a serious effect upon surface discolouration. Petrographic examination of samples of lichen-coated rock from sites in western New South Wales shows that humic acid, generated by lichen growth, attacks the quartz grains and permanently stains them green. A further point about surface coatings is the black soot deposits, presumably from camp-fires, which occur frequently in wet weather shelters and contribute to the obliteration of many painted figures.

The presence of moulds is not highly significant but does contribute to extensive damage at some sites. At Nourlangie there are examples of mould damage in the Nangaloar shelter and in caves adjacent to the main gallery of spirit figures. Paintings at Cannon Hill, the Cooper Creek area and at many other sites in the general region, are affected also by moulds. Provision of adequate drains to direct water away from shelters would prevent dampness and inhibit mould growth.

In some instances, the rocks in which shelters are situated are porous and water seeps through the walls, causing moulds on painted surfaces. Sometimes, water percolating through the rocks, dissolves and transports minerals from within and deposits them on the surface, causing fretting. Often paintings are badly affected, even though they are well away from exposed parts of shelters. In these circumstances it may be necessary to water-proof the outer surfaces to prevent entry of water.

Another factor to be taken into account is the high probability of changes in natural drainage brought about by rock-falls and earth movements. Some shelters which are now very damp may have been dry when they were occupied and painted. A good example is the group of rock engravings at the Hawk Dreaming site near Cannon Hill (Plate 40 bottom). The grooves abraded into the walls of this comparatively deep cave are heavily blackened with mould and staining. Water obviously rushes through the cave every time it rains, making it unsuitable for occupation. It is possible that at some time in the past the shelter was subjected to less water erosion.

155

Changes in drainage patterns brought about by rock-falls is a critical factor now that the art has been all but totally abandoned, due mainly to the extinction of the Aboriginal groups who owned and maintained the art sites of the region over many thousands of years.

Termite and Insect Damage

There are many examples of paintings almost totally obliterated by channels made across painted rock surfaces by white ants. Careful removal of the channels shows that the ochres beneath have been destroyed as a result of this activity.

The ants build nests in the ground at the base of the inner walls of shelters and work their way over the painted surfaces. As conditions vary, all shelters are not equally suited to termite infestation. The driest situations appear to be the least favoured, although there is some termite activity in almost every rock shelter. The amount of damage from this cause is a variable and dependant upon the particular environment of individual shelters.

Paintings in caves formed in large boulders fallen from the escarpment in Deaf Adder Creek Valley, are suffering extreme ant damage; many designs have been almost totally destroyed. These particular shelters seem to provide ideal conditions. Termites were active also at the main gallery. The nests at the base of the painted walls were treated with Dieldrin in 1972. This was effective immediately and the ants exterminated. The channels soon dried out and fell from the walls.

Mud wasps are yet another insect which cause considerable damage. They build quite large nests of wet mud over paintings. Although a variable, there are instances where wasps have built dozens of nests over paintings causing disfigurement to the art (Plate 38 bottom left). Swallows also build mud nests on the ceilings.

Animal Damage

The buffalo is yet another agent of destruction for the ancient rock art of the Alligator Rivers Region. After wallowing in thick, black mud, on the flats and in the water-holes, the buffalo tends to alleviate irritation by rubbing against a tree, rock or painted surface, if one happens to be nearby. The abrasive affect of fine gritty mud, backed by an enormous weight, sliding to and fro over delicate painted art works is all too obvious.

Since its introduction to the mainland in 1838 the buffalo has taken a significant toll of paintings in rock shelters at or near ground level. Leichhardt describes great numbers of buffalo on Cobourg Peninsula as early as 1845, and doubtless they soon spread south into the

Alligator Rivers Region. There is no doubt that since about 1850, the Aborigines had to contend with this interference to their sites. As a result, the amount of re-touching needed, particularly at sacred sites, might well have increased.

Paintings badly damaged by buffaloes have a wide distribution; the series of galleries in weathered boulders along the base of the escarpment at Deaf Adder Creek Valley have suffered substantial damage. Others at Cannon Hill have been similarly affected and also those in the Tin Camp Creek, Mt Borrodaile, Cooper Creek regions (Plate 39).

Many paintings bear evidence of abrasion by wild pigs and horses which also find shelter among the rock outcrops and overhangs along the base of the escarpment. In more inaccessible places and even isolated situations, wallabies, kangaroos and goats contribute to the overall damage.

It is of interest that the superintendent of Oenpelli Mission made regular use of caves '. . . which had all the drawings . . .' to house his goats during the wet season (Dyer 1934: 15, 26).

There is a simple remedy for this massive interference with sites; erection of strong fences to prevent use of shelters by animals. There is an abundance of unpainted overhangs and caves where game can shelter without doing harm.

Mechanical Weathering

Plants, shrubs and even trees take root in crevices during the summer wet season when rocks become saturated. Often this occurs high up on rock-faces and plants send down a network of roots on the outer surfaces and through cracks and faults in the rocks.

With successive years of growth some rocks are prised apart, opening the way to seepage. The root systems themselves can obliterate paintings; the damage they cause to the rock-face itself is a determining factor in the life of some paintings (Plate 41).

Removal of growth and also trees which have taken root at the base of rock walls, can easily avoid further damage. However, such action does sometimes contravene age-old tribal laws. While recording sites in the Cooper Creek region, I asked an Aboriginal companion to pull back a large bush to enable a series of obscured paintings to be photographed. He was terrified lest a branch should be broken. The leafy growth represented the 'beard of the ancestor of the cave'. Damage to the *Kundjawurrk* (whiskers) would mean certain reprisals against the individual concerned.

As the Aboriginal was not the owner of the cave and had agreed to supervise my visit only after Priscilla Marinyinginyi Giradbul (the hereditary owner) had given her consent, he would be held directly

157

Plate 41 Plant roots invade many shelters, clinging to the walls and prising open crevaces. Paintings at this site situated in a large boulder at the base of the escarpment in Deaf Adder Creek Valley, are certain to be destroyed in a few years.

responsible for any damage. There is little documentation of such instances, but there is no doubt that the intrusion of thoughtless non-Aboriginals into remote parts of Australia must have caused great concern among the indigenous people of different areas, particularly where interference to sacred sites was concerned. It may be that some seemingly unwarranted attacks by Aborigines were prompted by unwitting interference to places of sacred significance.

An early historic example of the impact of European actions was recorded by Petrie (1904: 254). In the 1840s his father went timber cutting with Aboriginal labour amongst the bunya pines of south-eastern Queensland. 'Arriving at the tree, they started to cut . . . and the blacks showed they did not like this at all.' Although Petrie only intended removing a section of timber, the Aborigines would not 'even cut notches in a bunya pine, and on this occasion they almost cried in their distress.'

It is important to note that my Aboriginal companion in the Cooper Creek region refused to be photographed with paintings appearing in the background. Even today, old taboos persist; a knowledge of them is important when considering future safeguards for art in regions where Aborigines are semi-traditionally oriented.

Critical damage to painted rock surfaces can be caused also by scaling due to temperature changes. Sometimes quite large pieces become dislodged and fall to the ground taking paintings with them. An example of this type of damage is illustrated on Plate 38 top right.

Bush fires are responsible also for fracturing many surfaces, some painted with designs. Often undergrowth around rock shelters is too sparse to ignite easily. In several seasons the growth accumulates until it becomes vulnerable, at which time it often catches alight and does irreparable damage. Clearing undergrowth from around caves would be a wise precaution and remove the possibility of unnecessary damage from this cause.

Sand Abrasion

The abrasive effects of wind-borne sand can be very drastic in some circumstances. There are instances, particularly at lower levels, where painted surfaces have been all but totally removed to a depth of several centimetres. Harder residual parts of the surface which have resisted weathering often bear fragments of paintings showing that whole panels of art at one time existed. An example of advanced damage from this cause was found at Birndu (*Ngarradj Warde Djobkeng*) where an extensive face has been cut into by erosion (Kamminga and Allen 1973: 29-32).

159

Construction of simple wind-breaks to deflect the force and direction of the wind could be a remedy to the problem.

Flaking Pigments

The Aborigines painted on some surfaces which are exposed to the full force of the sun's rays for at least part of the day. Although natural ochres do not fade, the intense heat and changes in temperature can cause pigments to flake.

The preparation and application of paint is a basic factor in the life of an ochre art work. Finely ground pigments carefully applied have a better chance of survival than hastily mixed ochres painted thickly on to the rock.

The main gallery at Nourlangie Rock (Plate 23) is known to have been re-painted in about 1962-63 (Attenborough 1963: 43-79). The pigments used were coarse and applied thickly, with the result that the figures have deteriorated rapidly. A photograph taken in 1965 (Plate 42 top) shows a section of a newly painted figure; there was obvious flaking of the paint work by 1973 (Plate 42 bottom).

Dust Damage

Air-borne dust is yet another menace to painted galleries. Prolonged Aboriginal occupation of many shelters has resulted in a natural floor of fine dust and ashes. Being dry, little growth occurs to bind the materials together. Wind whips up this fine powder and blows it on to the walls of caves, in some instances actually obliterating the paintings.

The situation is even more serious under conditions of high humidity, as the moisture laden air dampens the dust particles which then adhere to the rock surface to become an irremovable blanket over the surface. The Nangaloar cave at Nourlangie Rock has suffered badly from dust and in time most designs will disappear.

The opening of a road to Oenpelli in the late 1950s has brought an increasing amount of traffic into the general region. Fortunately, it is routed so as to be an insignificant factor as far as the cave art is concerned.

A more serious situation has developed where tourist access tracks extend to sites. This is quite a frequent occurrence although regular conducted tours are at present limited to two or three main caves, in

161

particular Nangaloar and Obiri Rock. Such tracks usually go right to the painted section of galleries and after continuous use become soft with the result that as each vehicle stops it sends a cloud of dust into the shelter. The position is even worse when tracks become much used roads, either to or passing unique galleries. This is the situation at Obiri Rock (Plate 43 bottom), where there is a regular traffic past the outstanding galleries. Dust rising from each vehicle finds its way into the shelter.

Vandalism

In most parts of Australia vandalism by thoughtless visitors to sites is a major cause of deterioration and destruction.

At the Laura Aboriginal galleries in Cape York photographers moistened paintings to make them stand out for photography. As a result, whole figures were washed from the walls. Trezise (1969: 47) has found that names are frequently written in charcoal on the Laura galleries to the detriment of the art.

Wright (1970: 125) describes paintings in Rio Tinto Gorge, seventy kilometres west of Wittenoom in Western Australia which are overlaid by initials and chalked figures. In another instance portion of an engraved face was blasted away with dynamite by a member of a road construction team.

In Queensland the same situation exists; a small site near Mt Elliott, south of Townsville, was completely destroyed by a road gang. Certain rock art sites also have been 'improved' by the addition of figures; other sites particularly in the Carnarvon Ranges, have been deliberately destroyed by over-painting (Colliver, 1970: 9-10).

At Ayers Rock lead based paints were sprayed over cave art while near Alice Springs, fragments of rock were levered and chiselled from an historic art site recorded in 1896 by Spencer. In South Australia one site was destroyed by a large painted advertisement which completely covered a series of ancient red ochre drawings (Ellis 1972: 53). Even in the depths of Koonalda Cave, vandals have scratched initials across the 20 000 year old wall markings.

Vandalism is not unique to Australia. In other countries extensive damage has been caused to rock art sites. In southern Africa, where there is a wealth of art painted by the Bushmen, the hunters and

162

gatherers of Africa, vandals have scrawled and scratched their names over and around paintings. Rudner and Rudner (1970: 262) relate how paint also has been splashed over ancient drawings and attempts made to chip them off. Careless and uncaring farmers have walled in large painted shelters for use as stock-yards. The greasy bodies of animals rubbing against rock-faces besmear and smudge paintings. Heat and smoke from fires of campers have also damaged and obliterated painted motifs. Thieves have attempted to chisel or blast paintings and engravings from rocks only to destroy them. In the past, hundreds of specimens have been sent from Africa to museums in Europe and elsewhere.

There is an account of a schoolteacher and her class, who, equipped with mops and buckets of water, attempted to wash 'rude and heathen' paintings from the rocks—fortunately the paint had penetrated well into the rock and their efforts to remove them were unrewarded.

Legislation to protect Bushman art was carried in 1911, 1923 and 1937. It is a punishable offence to damage or to remove, without permission, any painting or engraving or to excavate archaeological sites without a permit. However, in common with Australia, ignorance and apathy are widespread and inadequate policing of laws negate to a large extent the objectives of the legislative provisions.

Vandalism is not restricted to any one country or region. It is a universal problem which increases as new sites are discovered and made known and the public attains greater mobility in an age of affluence.

The only destructive forces prior to European settlement of Australia were the natural ones of wind and water. Designs pecked in hard rock are resistant to both types of erosion. As described earlier in this chapter, paintings in favourable positions, protected from rain by rock shelters and facing away from prevailing winds, have survived with the original brilliance of the colours intact.

It is not the Sunday 'beer-can-and-rifle' vandal who is the most destructive. Often it is the road constructor, the railway builders, dam engineers, pipeline construction gangs and town planners who contribute to massive destruction.

Grant (1972: 75-78) describes how developmental projects have taken enormous toll of sites in parts of the valleys of the Columbia and Colorado Rivers in the American South-west. Flooding of vast sections of these valleys destroyed hundreds of sites in one or two gigantic operations.

However, in the United States, there has been an increasing commitment to long-range salvage operations wherever a project threatens extensive archaeological material. When important sites

164

are endangered by road or pipe-laying operations, work is held up until the material can be examined and if necessary recovered by experts. The cost of the study and publication of the results are met by the company or government agency concerned.

The United States Federal and some State agencies have become increasingly concerned with the destruction of so many sites and plans are well underway to save something for future generations. Important sites have been incorporated into new National Parks where trails and roads are created to take visitors to rock art sites that are constantly under supervision.

At the state and local levels, a number of excellent attempts have been made to move threatened sites from their original positions, to the safety of higher ground beyond the water levels of new dams. Many property owners have taken the initiative and fenced sites and allow only supervised visits. A regular programme of recording and designation of sites as national landmarks is doing much to preserve an important part of American prehistory.

It is not unrealistic to believe that similar steps could be taken in the Alligator Rivers Region should development take place. However, the comparative inaccessibility of the Region until the last decade has minimised the instances of damage to art sites by vandals. It is refreshing to visit gallery after gallery and find the paintings unmarked by initials and lettering and few instances where portions of painted rock have been levered from the walls. Vandalism will only become a major problem if the region is made easily available to large numbers of people without adequate safeguards and specific protection to important sites.

Preservation of Art

Conservators agree on the nature of the factors contributing to the general deterioration of rock paintings; they agree also that continuous neglect will have serious consequences. Provision of adequate personnel to carry out the relatively straightforward procedures necessary to conserve sites is deserving of consideration by the appropriate authority.

Intensive urban development in many parts of Australia has resulted in the destruction of vast numbers of Aboriginal paintings. In the Alligator Rivers Region where painting continued as a part of the living culture of Aborigines until a much later period, there are opportunities to preserve examples of unique art styles.

It is important to involve Aborigines who retain links with the traditional past in any future plans to protect, preserve and develop sites.

They are the rightful owners of this heritage which could be preserved for all Australians and made available to people of all nations.

In the United States programmes are being developed to involve Indians in archaeological recording and conservation programmes. Sullivan (pers. comm.) found that one of the proposals being initiated by the Office of Indian Programmes, United States Department of the Interior, through the Arizona Archaeological Centre, is designed to facilitate the continuing development of Indian lands while at the same time providing for the conservation of the historic and archaeological heritage of the different tribal groups.

Such plans include provision for long-term, full-time employment of five to eleven Indians on each reservation in southern Arizona.

Employment involves considerable training and is designed to develop expert technicians in many facets of archaeological studies. Each employee is encouraged to develop to the limit of his or her abilities. The organisers feel that, given good selection of intelligent personnel and adequate motivation, it is reasonable to suppose that some may become interested enough to obtain the necessary academic background to assume some of the professional positions in the programme.

The proposal is to initially establish archaeological conservation teams to perform excavation and or survey tasks at five Indian reservations. The archaeological conservation teams are of three types: survey teams, excavation teams, and conservation teams (composed of a survey unit and an excavation unit). They are comprised of professional archaeological supervisors, a laboratory assistant, and five to ten archaeological assistants. Indians may fill any of the positions, however, there are few Indians qualified at this time to fill the professional positions.

Supervisors of conservation and excavation teams are required to be able to evaluate archaeological and historical resources and design research programmes to extract a maximum amount of data from sites. In addition, they must be able to train and communicate effectively with the teams. Timely reports on survey and excavation projects also are required.

Supervisors of survey teams are capable in archaeological survey, resource evaluation, and in conducting minor excavation projects. They are able to train and supervise survey team members.

Survey team (or unit) personnel are trained primarily in the recognition and recording of archaeological art and historic sites, collecting artifacts from these sites, map and aerial photograph reading, and the precise location and plotting of sites on maps. These tasks are performed with independence of direct supervision as personnel become proficient. They also perform, under direct supervision, small excavation projects.

Under direct supervision excavation team (or unit) personnel perform and are trained in increasingly responsible technical excavation tasks such as: excavating house floors, burials and other fragile remains; plane-table surveying, basic recording, collecting samples, stratigraphic testing, cleaning and preliminary sorting of specimens for analysis, preservation of specimens, photography, and preparing and recording profiles.

Laboratory assistants are trained in cleaning, preserving, repairing and labelling specimens, and preliminary sorting of specimens for analysis. Depending upon individual abilities, they are further trained in other curatorial functions, drawing specimens or maps and photography.

On all of the reservations for which teams are recommended, there are numerous archaeological resources which are endangered by an increasing rate of development.

The functions which the teams are expected to fulfill are to:

- Compile a complete inventory of archaeological and historical resources available to each tribal group.
- Recommend resources which merit permanent or long-term preservation of development to encourage tourism.
- Perform archaeological studies to furnish archaeological clearance for lands required for development. For large projects with a limited period of time to complete studies, additional solutions are sometimes required.
- Provide archaeological studies of sufficient depth to prepare adequate environmental impact statements.
- Provide information and specimens by means of which the tribal groups may develop an increased appreciation and awareness of their cultural heritage.
- Provide data to enable planners and decision makers for the tribal groups and the Bureau of Indian Affairs, to make intelligent selection of alternative courses of action in conjunction with projects which involve adverse effects upon archaeological and historical resources.
- Provide employment and job training for Indians on their own lands in useful and needed work.

In some instances the United States National Park Service funds, without reimbursement, studies required to provide archaeological clearance for tribal projects or on individual allotments. For programmes funded by the Bureau of Indian Affairs or other government agencies, these services are provided on a reimbursable basis. For private developments under leases, grants or other rights of privilege, full reimbursement is required when economically feasible. In other instances, the developers are required to meet a fair share of the costs.

Although the starting level for Indian personnel is low because of their lack of experience and background, the main objective of the programme is to train them and develop career ladders by which they can advance.

Similar opportunities could be created for Aboriginal involvement in site recording, conservation and research programmes, both within reserves and in all areas where sites of significance to Aborigines are located. The Alligator Rivers Region provides a unique situation where a great number of Aborigines could be involved on a full-time basis in the investigation and conservation of a vast array of sites of importance to all Australians and to mankind.

CHAPTER 6

Cultural Tourism

Australia, in common with other countries, has its heritage of antiquities, monuments and sites which have come down to the present generation with varying degrees of conservation and care. The preservation of this rich cultural legacy has become increasingly a matter of international concern, as some countries give low priority to the conservation of monuments and others lack the funds needed to implement a progressive programme aimed at preservation of a representative series of cultural sites.

As the survey has shown, Aboriginal art and archaeological sites in the Alligator Rivers Region rank high on the list of Australian sites and are an important part of Australia's cultural heritage. It is relevant to include consideration of their preservation, protection and development in any overall development plan. Before discussing specific possibilities an outline of procedures adopted in overseas countries may provide a useful background.

Monument Conservation in Britain

The British system of conservation of monuments provides one of the best illustrations of the scope of such activities in European countries. The preservation of ancient and historic sites is largely the responsibility of the Ministry of Public Building and Works, which is voted over $6m annually by Parliament for the acquisition, maintenance and development of monuments in England, Scotland and Wales.

The Act under which the Ministry functions defines the term 'ancient monument' very broadly. Potentially it includes almost any building or structure of historic interest of any kind, made or occupied by man, from ancient to modern times. The term, however, expressly

169

excludes ecclesiastical buildings in use, with the result that cathedrals, churches and some other structures used for church purposes fall outside the scope of the Ancient Monuments Act.

A directly employed staff of about 1 000 persons is engaged for the specific purpose of supervising the preservation of 12 000 scheduled monuments and 253 000 listed buildings. In England alone, during 1969, the extraordinarily large number of 281 sites were recommended for scheduling. In the same year more than twelve million people paid nearly $2m to visit the 700 monuments open to the public. A further three million people visited National Trust properties which are subsidized by the Ministry (National Trust Annual Report 1969: 34).

The number and range of monuments presents an enormous challenge to the Ministry's team of specialists, who seek constantly for new techniques to combat an increasing complexity of problems. The insidious effects of atmospheric pollution have created new dilemmas for which no satisfactory solution has been found. The Ministry has even purchased stone and lime quarries to ensure faithful restoration of the fabric of ancient masonry structures.

With 700 sites open for public inspection, special attention has been given to the development of monuments in a manner that ensures both protection and ready access. The famous *Stonehenge*, in Wiltshire, is a good example. In 1970 there was a dramatic increase in the number of visitors to this intriguing 4 500 years old monument and estimates of nearly one million people have been made for the immediate future. To cope with an average of perhaps 4 000 people per day during the summer season, new facilities have been provided, including increased provision for car parking, an underpass to avoid disruption to traffic and a special reception centre, sited below ground level to preserve the general environment (Plate 44 bottom).

When vulnerable sites of particular importance are in need of preservation, they are encompassed by a suitably designed building. An extensive late first century Roman palace discovered at Fishbourne in Sussex, in 1960, is a superb example of protection by this means. The Sussex Archaeological Trust, aided by Government grants, has incorporated the systematically excavated ruins of this outstanding Roman building in a site museum. Protection is assured

and the public has complete access to every feature of the monument. This museum complex includes a special display section made possible by a gift of $40 000 from *The Sunday Times*. Exhibits, sketches, plans and photographs show the history of the building materials used, construction methods and life in Roman Britain of the period. Artifacts found during many seasons of excavation are prominent in the displays.

Such elaborate development cannot be extended to every site, but the best examples are effectively preserved in this way. A less ambitious but equally adequate structure has been erected by the Ministry to protect the excavated remains of a Roman villa at Lullingstone in Kent (Plate 44 top).

The British realise that tourism is one of the fastest growing industries in the world. Despite fluctuating economic and political conditions, tourist traffic increased at levels between ten and sixteen percent annually between 1950 and 1956. It stabilized at a level of between six and ten percent between 1956 and 1960. During the 1960s, as a result of the rising national income of the industrialized countries, coupled with a corresponding rise in the standard of living, more leisure time and growth of population, international tourist flows again began to increase very rapidly.

Britain has been one of the major beneficiaries from the increase in the number of international tourists. During 1970, nearly seven million overseas visitors went to Britain and their total expenditure (excluding receipts from transport to and from Britain) amounted to over $433 million.

The number of visitors to Britain in 1969 was twenty-one percent higher than in 1968; the increase for the world in general and for Europe as a whole, was less than ten percent. In 1970, the number of visitors to Britain rose by nearly sixteen percent and the trend still continues (British Information Services 1972: 1-2).

One of the main magnets drawing visitors to Britain is its rich heritage of ancient monuments and sites. A similar cultural tourist industry could be developed in Australia around the unique relics of 30 000 years of Aboriginal history.

The figures for cultural tourism in the United States are even more impressive. Florida, one of the main tourist States, had 23 000 000 interstate and overseas visitors in 1970. They used 138 000 000 nights of accommodation and spent five billion seven hundred million dollars which returned to the Government of Florida alone in taxation $275 000 000. These figures are the ultimate in cultural tourism, but every country benefits in some way.

172

The French Monuments

Britain is not alone in its concerted effort to preserve a rich heritage of ancient monuments and develop them for tourists. Its neighbour, France, has some of the world's most interesting prehistoric art sites. The most dramatic of these great galleries is Lascaux in southern France. The walls of this impressive underground gallery teem with life. Huge bison, bulls, cows, horses, deer and ibex in different shades of red, yellow, brown and black form a sharp contrast with the pale background of the cave walls. The subjects of the paintings on the walls and ceiling of this great subterranean sanctuary presumably form part of the symbolic and magic beliefs of upper Palaeolithic hunting societies.

The closely kept secret of the cave was unlocked accidentally on 12th September, 1940 by Jacques Marsel (still a ranger at the site) and four young companions. The boys had lost their dog while hunting in the woods in the valley of the Vezere River near Montignac in the Dordogne. Muffled barks coming from a small hole where a large fir tree had fallen, led them into the cave and its richly coloured frescoes.

The French Government, quick to recognise that the Lascaux paintings were undoubtedly one of the world's greatest art treasures, surpassing all other examples of Ice Age art, proclaimed the site as an historic monument three months after its discovery. The cave was opened to the public following modifications to the entrance and installation of equipment to maintain the original atmosphere by controlling temperature, humidity and carbon dioxide concentrations.

People flocked from all over the world to see this 'Pre-historic Sistine Chapel', as it became known. Numbers increased to 125 000 each year and the local district benefited greatly from an expansion of cultural tourism.

The size and frequency of the parties kept the air conditioning units working at full capacity, and the rapidly circulating air caused contamination of the walls. A crisis was reached in September, 1960, when green patches began to appear, posing a threat to the paintings. A special commission was appointed by the French Minister of Cultural Affairs, comprising a score of specialists—biologists, geologists, speleologists and archaeologists who were charged with taking effective measures to safeguard the paintings.

Despite heavy financial loss, the cave was immediately closed to the public and exhaustive studies undertaken to identify the malady. An algal infection was found to have been introduced into the cave by workmen who modified the entrance and passageways for public

Plate 45 In the Dordogne of France archaeological and prehistoric art sites are developed for public viewing. This site situated in an extensive rock shelter near Les Eyzies attracts many thousands of overseas visitors each summer. Cases display stone and bone tools recovered in the deposits together with explanations of their age and significance.

access. The position was aggravated by the entry of large numbers of visitors who brought into the cave great quantities of organic substances such as pollen, breath, sweat and bacteria, enabling the algae to spread. Effective remedies were evolved and the infection eradicated without damage to the paintings. (Lefevre and Laporte 1969: 35-44). Alteration to the atmospheric conditions also induced the growth of calcite crystals on the walls.

The positive attitude of the French authorities saved the art of Lascaux for mankind. The cave is now partially re-opened and each year a small number of scientists are permitted entry to study the art. It is hoped eventually to make the paintings available again to the public, but before this can be considered, a means must be found to isolate visitors from the paintings. In the meantime a replica of the underground gallery is being constructed at the site for interested tourists.

Lascaux is by no means the only fresco cave in the picturesque Vezere Valley. Indeed the region is rich in sites. The charming village of Les Eyzies lies in the centre of this region and is one of numerous towns which thrive on the tourist industry built around prehistoric sites. Among the many large caves containing superb examples of Palaeolithic paintings and engravings are Font-de-Gaume and Les Combarelles, both accessible to the public. The cliffs lining the river valleys are studded with rock shelters and caves which contain deep deposits of occupation debris left by successive populations over some 30 000 years.

Numerous excavations carried out for more than a century have yielded a wealth of relics and data, enabling reconstruction of the prehistoric pattern of life in this region. Sites have been tastefully developed for public access and are manned by knowledgeable guides. Site museums protect excavation sections and display representative collections of stone and bone tools, faunal remains and portable art objects (Plate 46).

Development is planned always to ensure harmony with the local environment. Structures are not necessarily elaborate or expensive. In some instances archaeological sites are protected by simple screens and fences. The classic Mousterian site, discovered in 1863, is a good example of an inexpensive but adequate structure erected to prevent weather from damaging exposed deposits.

Involvement of UNESCO

At an international level, the UNESCO organization is accepting an increasing role in co-ordinating the work of experts in many fields of monument conservation. International co-operation facilitated the enormous task of re-siting the Nubian temples in upper Egypt, when they were threatened by the rising waters of the Aswan Dam. One of the many other projects being undertaken by UNESCO is the restoration of the great Borobudur temple in central Java. In the future there are likely to be an increasing number of projects in which international specialists combine their expertise to find solutions to major conservation problems.

A series of guidelines for monument conservation has been recommended by UNESCO. It considers that every country should ensure the protection and development of immovable cultural property by initiating exhaustive scientific, historical and artistic studies.

As part of its policy for international co-operation UNESCO has arranged seminars to focus attention on the problems arising from the accelerated deterioration of monuments due to natural weathering and to air and water pollution. The increasing quantity of fossil fuels being used by modern industry, generates dangerous levels of destructive sulphur oxides. Deposits both on stone and held in the upper atmosphere, combine with rain water to form sulphuric acid. This highly reactive liquid produces a chemical change in some types of stone, eventually destroying them. Such destruction threatens the noblest of the world's monuments in many countries, but it is not likely to be a major factor in Arnhem Land where the rocks are, in the main, sandstones and quartzites which generally resist the effects of atmospheric pollution.

As previously outlined, deterioration of Aboriginal rock art is due to many variable factors and a remedy to all the problems will not be simple. If answers are to be found to the many complex questions involved, scientific studies under local conditions are essential. Emphasis will need to be placed on recruitment and training of the qualified personnel, notably laboratory specialists, engineers, architects and archaeologists, needed to elaborate and supervise conservation programmes. Co-ordination of activities is necessary between all relevant local, regional and national services. If major monuments and sites are kept in good repair, it should avoid recourse to the costly operations imposed by major dilapidation.

UNESCO is willing to supervise research by international teams of specialists into pilot projects for the conservation of monuments and sites agreed to be of universal significance, and secures the widest possible dissemination of the results. UNESCO also will organize, in co-operation with other international organizations, seminars and meetings at international and regional levels, calculated to promote the application of the principles and techniques of conservation in light of local needs (Edwards 1972: 97-115).

It is apparent that the current international movement to preserve the world's antiquities has implications for the Alligator Rivers Region, where depth studies of the problems associated with the preservation of cave art could be considered by the appropriate government authority.

Ancient Monuments in Australia

In Australia, the range of monuments, antiquities and sites is extremely wide. Unique relics of 30 000 years and more of prehistory, in the form of cave paintings, rock engravings, carved trees, stone arrangements, settlement sites, and quarries, are scattered throughout the continent. Like their European counterparts, these monuments have been continually subjected to the variable factors of mechanical and chemical weathering. Earth tremors, flood, fire, attack by salt damp and moulds and, to a much lesser degree, atmospheric pollution, are but some of the agents of destruction that have taken a toll.

To date, little effort has been made to ensure that representative examples of surviving monuments are preserved and handed on to future generations. The Aboriginal cave art of north Australia, including the Alligator Rivers Region, is an example. Some sites may by ranked as of world significance in the realm of art. Yet such 'Lascaux galleries' of Australia are under massive attack, and preservation of an adequately representative selection merits serious consideration.

There is a fundamental difference between conservation attitudes in Australia and Europe. In most countries, there is a determination to preserve and develop monuments. The authorities responsible seem to be in no doubt about the best procedures to cope with the problems. Methods adopted are decided from an objective study of the site and its environment. Expertise is available through well-trained officers who are dedicated to the task of conservation. When development is complete suitably worded signs are erected to provide precise information to enable visitors to find the site and learn details of its history.

By comparison in Australia, there are few trained conservators, few objective studies and, to date, a lack of funds to finance adequate conservation and developmental projects. A fundamental difference in attitude also exists. In many overseas nations, there is an unbroken line to link present generations with populations of the recent and distant past, who are therefore able to identify with prehistoric monuments. National pride ensures their preservation; cultural tourism provides an added incentive. White Australians do not see such a continuity with Aboriginal antiquities in Australia, and their conservation usually has been relegated to low priority.

Despite Australia's late entry into this field, steps have been taken recently to establish administrative procedures and a system of grants, to assist the work.

The Australian Institute of Aboriginal Studies is undertaking a national programme to record Aboriginal sites. These are being recorded in a National Register of Sites. The work has high priority due to the increasing tempo of development throughout Australia and its destructive effects upon sites of traditional and historic importance to Aborigines.

The aim of the programme is to identify and record sites of special significance to Aborigines and also sites in areas where traditionally oriented groups no longer survive. It is recognized by the Institute, that it is the responsibility of the Commonwealth and State instrumentalities to protect sites so revealed and assessed.

Action to record and to obtain the protection of sites has the general support of Aborigines throughout Australia. The Institute intends that all field work directed towards the compilation of the Register should be carried out with the active co-operation of those Aborigines with traditional involvement in the matters under investigation.

The Institute's policy is that most investigation and recording should be done by, or under the control of, the different authorities responsible for the protection of sites in the Australian States and Territories.

In order to expedite and facilitate this work by those authorities, the Institute is making grants for specified studies and surveys to be made. Grants can also be made to individuals for special recording programmes where these are sponsored by, and carried out under the general supervision of, the relevant responsible authority.

In order to assess applications and to advise the Institute upon their funding, a Committee for Sites of Significance has been formed of the following representatives:
• one nominee of each State Relics Authority
• one representative of the Northern Territory Authority responsible for site protection
• at least one initiated Aboriginal nominated by the National Aboriginal Consultative Committee
• a representative of the Department of Aboriginal Affairs
• two social anthropologists nominated by the Advisory Committee on Social Anthropology
• one linguist nominated by the Linguistic Advisory Committee.

In addition to any special terms recommended by the Advisory Committee or the Institute's consultants, it is a condition of grants that each site investigated and reported should be described in a uniform manner. Quarterly progress reports are being made, including copies of maps, photographs and plans of studies completed during that quarter. Funded authorities (or individuals acting under their supervision) have undertaken to abide by the Institute's policy statement on secret/sacred material or any condition laid down by the Aborigines traditionally concerned (Australian Institute of Aboriginal Studies 1973, [Doc/No. 73/1373 A]). Investigation and depth studies of sites in the Alligator Rivers Region could be keyed into this system, through the Museums and Art Galleries of the Northern Territory.

Tourism in Australia

The international Union of Official Travel Organisations states that there were 181 million international tourist arrivals throughout the world in 1971; they spent an estimated $US 20 billion. The Pacific area's share was a mere three percent. This seems insignificant in view of the fact that Europe gains three-quarters of the world tourism, but it is growing at a rapid rate. The Boeing Company has a need to watch developments in world tourism. Their latest statistics show that the Pacific area had nearly six million arrivals in 1970, a doubling of visitations over the previous four years. By 1975 it is expected the number of arrivals in the Pacific will jump to over fourteen million and to double again to nearly thirty million by 1980.

Overseas visitors to Australia in 1972 totalled 426 403, an increase of nearly ten percent over the 1971 figure. In 1972 the Commonwealth Statistician's Balance of Payments credit on items listed under *Travel* which reflects visitor expenditure information, amounted to $129 million, a two percent increase over the 1971 figure. Although growth rates slowed down in 1972 an examination of past figures reveals an average annual increase of sixteen percent. By projecting this figure, the Australian Tourist Commission estimates that the travel industry will earn $574 million by 1980 (Washington 1972: 120)

Ayers Rock — Mt Olga National Park

With increasing affluence, mobility, leisure time and numbers of people, public use of national parks is growing in Australia as it is throughout the world. This trend is likely to be emphasised at the Ayers Rock-Mt Olga National Park, despite the relative isolation, because of growing recognition of its national and international significance.

179

In the holiday year 1960/61, 4 332 persons were admitted to the National Park. By 1964/65 the number had increased to 10 427 and in 1970/71 to 30 201. During August and September, 1972, entry fees to the Park were paid by 10 427 people, despite restrictions on travel resulting from a nationwide oil strike and road closures due to flooding.

On the assumption that certain improvements take place it is estimated that by 1980 the annual number of visitors will increase fivefold to 150 000. (Harris, Kerr, Forster and Co. 1969: 37).

Visitors to the Park are not restricted to any particular class of people but four main categories are of particular significance:

- school or college groups on essentially educational tours travelling by hire coaches, sleeping outdoors or in tents and controlled by teachers or other adults;
- family groups resident in Australia, travelling on extended holidays by private car, commonly sleeping in tents and more rarely in motel/hotels;
- groups of mature or elderly people travelling on tours organized by coach companies and generally sleeping in motels/hotels, although some companies provide safari camps with varying degrees of sophistication for the more adventurous or less wealthy; and
- individuals or families travelling to the Park by the regular Alice Springs-Ayers Rock air service, or by private plane, staying at a motel/hotel and depending for local travel on hiring a vehicle at Ayers Rock or on tours organized by motel/hotels.

International visitors constitute about ten percent of the total. Compared with other parts of Australia caravans are rare, possibly because of the poor condition of the roads and the long travel distances involved.

In 1970/71, seventeen percent (5 143) of all visitors arrived by aircraft, twenty-nine percent (8 666) by private motor vehicle and fifty-four percent (16 392) by coach. The comparable figures for the period 17th August to 8th September, 1972, are aircraft three percent, private motor vehicle twenty-six percent, and coach seventy-two percent. The increased percentage of entrants by coach, compared with the annual figures, probably results from studies being confined to the peak tourist period of the school holidays, when the number of junior visitors exceeded that of adults because of the many school or college coach tours.

Visitors in all categories share a common interest in the main attractions of the Park and frequently join together in recreational activities e.g. in climbing Ayers Rock or going on tours of the Aboriginal painting sites guided by the Curators. Nevertheless, their requirements in terms of accommodation, roads, and services provided by the Park staff vary greatly as do their environmental impact. To some extent conflicts of interest arise. Thus motel/hotel dwellers living in expensive accommodation may be upset by conditions in nearby camps as viewed from the motel/hotel windows and grounds (Ovington *et al.* 1973: 19-20).

Planning for the future development of Ayers Rock National Park is likely to take into account this type of growth and allow for even higher growth rates which will follow road improvements which are taking place.

Potentially, the Aboriginal could participate effectively in the development and operation of Ayers Rock-Mt Olga National Park, to the advantage of himself, the Park administration and the visitor. But this potential can be fully realized only if the right conditions exist and only over an extended period of time. Any approach to involvement of Aborigines in the Park should be based on the premise that the primary objective is enhancement of the Aborigines' situation with tourism as the secondary benefactor.

There are several aspects of the Park's development and operation in which the natural interests and abilities of Aborigines could be utilized if the proper organization and training were provided:

• **Presentation of Attractions** —

A major aspect of Ayers Rock is its Aboriginal significance. Aboriginal guides would have a greater depth of understanding of traditional cultural patterns and could relate these to the Aboriginal use of the Rock. Aborigines with their intimate knowledge of the landscape would help as trail guides. They could also demonstrate the manufacture and use of different artifacts.

• **Entertainment**

Great potential exists for the development of performances of traditional Aboriginal music and dancing.

• **Arts and Crafts Production and Sales**

Although the primary outlets for arts and crafts will be in Alice Springs, the resort at Ayers Rock could support at least one shop.

• Other areas suggested was Park and Resort Development and Resort and Park Operation (Harris, Kerr, Forster and Co. 1969: 85-87).

Development of Aboriginal Sites for Tourism

Sydney Harbour, the Opera House, Canberra, the Great Barrier Reef, Ayers Rock, Australia's people and Aboriginal culture, are all outstanding tourism experiences. The rich Aboriginal art galleries and sites of the Alligator Rivers Region combined with picturesque escarpment country and large colonies of water birds, are one of the important tourist resources of the Nation.

In developing sites for tourism, it is desirable that appropriate controls are applied before damage occurs. Just as remoteness no longer ensures protection of Aboriginal sites, neither does it reduce their tourist appeal. Urban dwellers are motivated to escape into the 'empty wilderness', and transport technology has given them a means of reaching the remotest of sites. Four-wheel drive coaches are a common sight in central Australia. The noisy trail bike gives even more flexibility.

Conservation of sites selected for tourist usage would need to include developments which will provide a 'total environment for tourism'. Thought needs to be given to appropriate placement of reception points, camping facilities, picnic sites, and car parking areas. Visitors should be channelled along designated pathways to avoid destruction of the vegetation surrounding sites. Of central importance is the provision of public education programmes. This could start in schools and be continued at sites with interpretative displays, suitable notices and well-informed guides. Aborigines may be willing to accept a leading role in such cultural enterprises.

In the Alligator Rivers Region there are two areas which might be seriously considered for development as cultural museums; Nourlangie Rock, with its vast number of caves and picturesque environment, and the Cannon Hill-Obiri Rock complex of shelters. The art in these areas is extremely rich and representative of the main styles of the region. There are numerous archaeological deposits to provide for display, examples of the stone tools used over many thousands of years; systematic study of sites would ensure detailed data on the prehistory of Aboriginal occupation. Establishment of museums in these areas, showing Aboriginal cultural life and the history of contact, could do much to satisfy the interested public and ensure the protection of sites. It could provide also an industry for local Aborigines.

During a recent visit to the United States Sharon Sullivan of the New South Wales National Parks and Wildlife Service (pers. comm.) found great interest among National Park authorities in development of historic and cultural resources on Indian reservations in close co-operation with the local communities.

Among the ambitious plans being considered is a proposal involving the Pueblo of Zuni on the Zuni Reservation in New Mexico.

In accordance with the Zuni Comprehensive Development Plan, prepared in 1969, the Zuni-Cibola National Cultural Park is being planned to assist the Zuni people in presenting aspects of their culture and history to visitors. Particular attention is to be given to the interaction between the Pueblo culture and non-native groups. Programmes will focus on preservation and interpretation of the living culture and preservation and interpretation of selected historical remains.

The park will attempt to achieve the following objectives—

Visitor use: Encourage visitors to explore the present aspects of Zuni culture—their activities, ceremonies, crafts and villages—and also the historic sites, which will broaden the understanding of this ancient culture. Emphasise the desire of the Zuni people to retain their cultural integrity and still enjoy the advantages of twentieth century conveniences. Provide convenient facilities that will encourage visitors to remain in the area in order to appreciate the full range of activities and cultural events.

Management: Administer selected historical and archaeological sites directly. Supply advisory services for management, interpretation and protection of recreational, cultural and archaeological sites which the Zuni tribe would develop. Provide training for interested members of the community in operating, interpreting and preserving the resources. Give members of the Zuni tribe preferential treatment in management of the entire park operation, though the park would still retain its National Park Service status. This is a long-range goal. Emphasise that all reservation development programmes should be directed towards the maintenance of the integrity and local character of Zuni culture. Interest State agencies and local communities in promotional enterprises to increase visitation to the Zuni Reservation. Co-operate with other Federal agencies involved in implementing the Zuni Comprehensive Development Plan.

Research: Introduce research projects which will support National Park Service and Zuni interpretative programmes in history, archaeology and ethnology.

Resource preservation: Excavate and stabilize selected ruins. Restore and maintain the historic character of the Zuni Pueblo. Maintain Ojo Caliente as a late nineteenth century farming village.

Collections: Assemble archaeological specimens representing the material culture of people from the major prehistoric periods, emphasising those artifacts indicative of trade, technological change, the influx of new peoples into the Zuni country, and the welding of separate traditions into the distinctively Zuni tradition. Collect ethnological specimens from the historic period, representing both the conservative traditions of Zuni life and the introduction of European techniques. Collect artifacts associated with the late nineteenth century farming villages. Acquire a limited, highly selective collection of outstanding examples of nineteenth and twentieth century Zuni crafts.

Display of sacred objects: No artifacts, either prehistoric or historic, having symbolic or religious significance to the Zuni will be collected; no collection containing such artifacts will be displayed, except upon assurances of Zuni religious leaders that the collection or display of such items is in no way objectionable to the Zuni people. This same restriction will apply to facsimilies of religious paraphernalia.

To assist the Zuni tribe in the preservation of its cultural and historical resources the National Park Service has offered to assist in the following areas:
• Direct management of nationally significant historic and archaeological sites.
• Consultation with the Zuni authorities concerning preservation of the historic character of the inhabited villages and development of recreation resources.
• Training for members of the Zuni community in interpretation and park management.

Cultural tourist ventures of the kind outlined are being given high priority in the United States. Developments of a similar nature have validity in the Australian situation and may be relevant to the Alligator Rivers Region.

In the event of consideration being given to such developments it would be appropriate to commission feasibility studies to assess priorities and to examine the potential of particular sites for development as living museums.

The Deaf Adder Creek Valley region might more appropriately be considered as a scientific reserve for depth studies in art and archaeology as some sixty sites have been found already in the valley and adjacent plateau area. The date of 19 000 years ago, obtained for the Lindner gallery is one of the earliest dates associated with rock art sites anywhere in the world. (Kamminga and Allen 1973: 95). The likelihood of even earlier evidence marks the region as one of great interest to art historians.

The remoteness of Deaf Adder Creek Valley, its comparative inaccessibility, the general excellent condition of the art in its complex of sites and its potential for further archaeological investigations, makes it an area of particular importance. In view of this it would be desirable to consider special provisions in respect of this region.

Oenpelli itself is a potential tourist attraction but any development in this area would be a community matter.

A statement written in Britain nearly seventy years ago (Brown 1905: 1, 26) almost a century after Britain began serious consideration of monument preservation, is pertinent to the situation in Australia today. Ancient monuments, the writer said, 'embrace all old buildings and other memorials of bygone days. They are heirlooms from the past and appeal to the piety and patriotism of the present. Their number can never be increased, but on the contrary as time goes on they must necessarily become fewer. As the decay or destruction of any one of them involves an increase of value in those that endure, so the care of them will become every year a matter of more and more urgent duty.

'. . . coming developments in public life may give to the historic monument a worth we can hardly now realize. Whatever may be the future in other respects . . . it must always remain the soil in which are rooted all the traditional memories of the past . . . Some of the most urgent pleas for protection come now not from professed amateurs of the beautiful, but from men of affairs, and from active civic officials, who are alarmed at the sacrifices which are being made on every side to the exigencies of the present.'

Summary

The Review Report of the Alligator Rivers Environmental Fact Finding Study (Part 3: 1-17) summaries three important components of the Aboriginal cultural heritage in the Alligator Rivers Region: Aboriginal sites of significance, archaeological sites and rock art. The following extracts from the report provide a background to the detailed report on the rock art of the Region.

Aboriginal Sites of Significance

It is known that many landscape features and locations have or did have considerable sacred or mythological significance to living Aborigines and should therefore be regarded with respect and given due attention in any development plan.

Identifying sites of significance is not a straight-forward procedure. The existence or nature of some sites is a secret not revealed at all, or at most to a few in the strictest confidence; even then, information may be progressively revealed.

It is clear that to protect sites of significance, advice is necessary from Aborigines whose traditional rights may be concerned with specific areas. Because of the changes in the original tribal distributions within the Region, there are problems in determining which individuals possess the relevant affiliation with certain sites.

As the Department of Aboriginal Affairs possesses detailed information on many sites, and its officers have the confidence of many Aborigines, and know their likely whereabouts, adequate consultation with Aborigines seems most appropriate through that Department whenever developments are proposed.

Specialist source papers made available to the Study by the Department of Aboriginal Affairs and Peter Carroll of Oenpelli, illustrate clearly the effort necessary to identify appropriate informants in order to locate and explain particular sites.

186

Aborigines belong to territorial clans, membership being passed from father to children. It is amongst the clan members under a particular clan name that individuals may be found who are knowledgeable and interested in matters concerning the land within their clan territories. These territories do not correspond to cadastrally surveyed portions of land. They are more akin to clusters of sites which are of particular significance to the clan. There are no distinct boundaries to the territories. Clan borders should be regarded as corridors rather than well-defined lines comparable to state borders. The clan territory and their bounds are determined by conspicuous natural features—rock outcrops, waterholes, rivers, etc.— that have economic or purely legendary, but more often mythototemic significance. Within the last mentioned category are the 'sacred-dangerous' sites which are often known beyond the borders of a particular clan. The delineation of borders is thus complicated by the fact that certain 'sacred' sites or ceremonial grounds are shared by several, not necessarily adjoining clans. This can result in apparently contradictory attributions unless the complex clan affiliations are understood by the investigator.

In Aboriginal tradition there were no 'paramount chiefs'. Instead there were recognised leaders, initiated men who were 'experts', for each aspect of communal activity. Similarly there was no one administrative border of the clan territory; instead, interclan activities (economic, religious, ceremonial) created overlapping spheres of influence. More than one clan therefore may be concerned with the same site. For this reason there are difficulties in identifying those who are most directly concerned with specific areas.

Most natural features have Aboriginal names. The majority are the equivalent of European geographical names. Some refer to favoured hunting, food gathering, and camping places. Others have legendary significance. This category includes 'Dreaming-places' of a non-sacred nature. The most important sites are those of mythototemic significance—places where great ancestral beings emerged from the ground, where they are now said to reside, and features these mythical beings created during the 'Dreamtime'. Some of these sites are considered to be 'sacred' and/or 'dangerous'; that is present-day Aborigines entirely avoid approaching them for fear of being killed, contracting diseases, or causing natural catastrophies, such as rock falls or floods, they hesitate to reveal information about them.

Many of these 'sacred' and/or 'dangerous' sites are connected with the Rainbow Snake or Serpent, one of the most powerful creator beings. Well-established mythology is associated with some sites; summaries are provided in the source papers for a number of sites in the Nabarlek and Mt Brockman areas. These explain both the existence of prominent natural features, their association with the people whose territory they are in, and the sacredness and awe in which they are held.

It needs to be emphasised that only the Aborigines for whom a particular site holds ceremonial or clan revelance, are those able to provide details of its location and importance. Information may be revealed progressively, after the enquirer has won the confidence of the informants. However, the extent of some sites is often difficult to define because of the fear of informants to go close to them. This in itself indicates the importance with which they are regarded by the Aborigines.

The source papers and other anthropological writings, indicate that the attitude of the Aborigines to many of the sites recorded by Europeans, is that they are afraid of any interference, such as disturbance of ground, trees or other associated features; even noise is held to be dangerous in some instances.

Archaeological Sites

When the Australian Aborigines first arrived in Australia, it is likely that they came in through north Australia hence this region has special interest to the archaeologist.

It is known that the Alligator Rivers Region was richly endowed environmentally from the point of view of Aboriginal people in the past.

A study of the archaeological resources of the region was made by special consultants—H. R. Allen and J. Kamminga. They did not attempt to locate all sites but to sample areas to determine the status of sites in each.

Sites at Mt Brockman and Tin Camp Creek Valley were examined but not excavated because of the concern of Aborigines in regard to disturbance of soil.

Most sites studied cluster around the plateau outliers particularly between Cannon Hill and Djawumba massif and in Deaf Adder Creek Valley, one of the large valleys within the plateau area. There is less concentration of sites on the escarpment face probably because of less suitable cave and shelter development. Studies were also made of a limited number of sites on the flood-plain.

Eighty sites were examined on the plateau outliers to the west and north of the main escarpment. The existence of shelter, and access to a range of environmental resource zones such as cliff and plateau, estuarine rivers and lagoons, freshwater lagoons and alluvial plains, accounts for the intensive use of these outlier sites. Archaeological deposits are well preserved. It is in this region that evidence has been obtained of settlement in north Australia some 20 000 to 25 000 years BP.

Valleys within the plateau, Tin Camp Creek Valley, and Deaf Adder Creek Valley, contain important sites. The first was examined earlier by Carmel White, when a student at the Australian National University. She excavated two sites and identified them as manufacturing centres for stone tools, occupied in the wet season. The lower sites near Cannon Hill, also occupied in the wet, were found to be places for the manufacture of wood, bone and shell artifacts, and for repairing weapons, using stone components made elsewhere.

At least one 20 000 years old site occurs in the Deaf Adder Creek Valley. It is the oldest plateau site yet excavated and contains a high density of artifacts and a large percentage of pieces of ochre. However, the site lacks the organic remains found in outlier sites. Seventeen sites were recorded in this valley.

Twelve sites were located on the flood-plains, including two stone arrangements on Munmarlary station and ten surface camp-sites on the edge of lagoons. The latter are subject to flooding and hence could have been occupied only in the dry season. They appear to have been exposed initially by the trampling of buffaloes, and subsequently damaged by them. The tool types found suggest that these sites may be some 7 000 years old.

The study confirmed that many sites with archaeological data of high value exist in the region. More than 120 sites were recorded. Some contain occupational deposit two metres or more deep and seven sites have now been shown by radiocarbon dating to be 10 000-25 000 years old. These represent the earliest known settlements in tropical Australia and have provided the world's oldest evidence for the technology of grinding stone for axes and also the oldest grindstones in Australia.

Because archaeological material is so well preserved at some sites, including organic material, the region has the potential for studying prehistoric economy and subsistence behaviour over a continuous time span from the Pleistocene epoch to the present.

The possibility of reconstructing past Aboriginal society makes the region important not only to Australian archaeology but also to world archaeology. Further, interpretation of past environmental evidence can be of value to other scientific studies.

The wide range of past and present environmental conditions makes it possible to study Aboriginal use of, and adaptation to, different environments. The dual use of two or more environments is already evident, e.g. plateau outliers and the adjacent plains.

The existence of numerous well-preserved galleries of Aboriginal art of considerable antiquity at these same sites makes it possible to study art in association with archaeological history.

There are many detailed records of early European contact with Aborigines in this region, and good collections of specimens of their material culture were preserved. Hence there is scope to correlate these with archaeological remains.

Some important sites have been damaged by animals and/or human agencies. Once disturbed the sites lose value for chronological or comparative studies.

Two sites at Birndu, near the proposed access road from the Arnhem Highway, could become vulnerable to public access when the new road is constructed. One is the largest site yet found in western Arnhem Land.

In some burial sites, skeletons are exposed. Many have already been stolen and others are endangered by vandalism.

At present mining activities do not occur on any known archaeological or art sites. Further, sites located near these activities have been protected by strict policy instructions to mining company staff and the appointment of additional rangers. However, if mining proceeds, and a local townsite is developed, the increased numbers of people in the vicinity, many of whom will not be responsible to the mining companies, will mean that the accessible and transportable relics will be in ever increasing danger, unless further protective measures are taken.

Some archaeological sites are of such scientific importance that consideration of their protection for future studies is warranted. This applies particularly to sites in the Cannon Hill and Deaf Adder Creek Valley areas.

Selected excavation sites, together with adequate areas of the associated environments actually exploited by the Aborigines and combined with examples of Aboriginal art, could be valuable for educational and tourist purposes.

Aboriginal Art Sites

The existence of Aboriginal rock art in the region has been known since the 1880s when Cahill of Oenpelli fame first visited the area. Further descriptions were given by Stockdale, Spencer, Dyer, Tindale, McCarthy and others but the first detailed study was made by Mountford, leader of the American-Australian Scientific Expedition of 1948.

The present survey recorded over 300 sites and provides the most extensive descriptions and photographic coverage yet available.

Although the sites are distributed widely from north to south they, like the archaeological sites, are concentrated on the escarpment and outliers of Kombolgie sandstone where numerous all-weather rock shelters occur in close proximity to varied and plentiful food resources. Aborigines have occupied these sites for thousands of years and as art was an integral part of Aboriginal life a rich heritage of rock art has been the consequence.

Not only are the galleries of paintings numerous, many are of extremely high quality. In 1956 Mountford, a recognized authority in this field, described the Oenpelli cave paintings as being more skilfully executed and more varied in design than those of any other part of Arnhem Land, and as the most numerous and beautiful series of cave paintings known in Australia. Other excellent galleries are described in this report.

Aboriginal rock art is of several different styles: at most sites in the Alligator Rivers Region monochrome dark red paintings underlie the more elaborate polychrome art. These figures are of animals and human forms and are often very large representations. Some can be described as a primitive or early form of X-ray art. This is the earliest style in the region and has a distribution far beyond the area under survey.

Mimi art is a very old, animated style in which stick-like figures in varied action postures depict battle and hunting scenes in large complex compositions, usually in monochrome red. Thirty or more figures occur in some friezes on vertical walls. Weapons and artifacts are shown and as these paintings are of considerable antiquity they constitute a pictorial history of considerable value for detailed study. For example, some earlier paintings show spears being used as javelins, later ones demonstrate the change to the spear-thrower in use. This style of art was apparently lost at some unknown time in the past and paintings of this kind are thought by Aborigines to be painted by spirit people called *Mimi*.

X-ray art is static; the artist depicting not only the outline of his subject but also what he knows to be inside. It has been practised in many countries but reached its highest level in Arnhem Land. Subjects depicted are mostly animals, with barramundi, catfish and other species very common; turtles, kangaroos, crocodiles, snakes, and goannas. It is a polychrome form with yellow, red and white most common. The paintings reveal internal organs such as skeletons, heart, lungs, stomach and intestines. The human figure is rarely painted in this form.

Besides the *Mimi* and X-ray styles which predominate at most sites, there are large numbers of stylised human figures. These are sometimes quite large and may be animated or in static form. Hand stencils also occur frequently.

Beeswax figures, made of wax pressed on to the rock-face, occur at many sites. Rock engravings were found at only one location, Lightning Dreaming in Sawcut Gorge, although there are occurrences of large grinding grooves at Hawk Dreaming and at Cannon Hill. At Deaf Adder Creek Valley ancient cup-shaped hollows, pounded into the cliff-face underlie the paintings.

Culture contact art occurs at most sites but is more common nearer the coast. Subjects represented were not part of the Aborigines normal life but arose out of early visits by Macassan fishermen, European expeditions and such events as the building of the Pine Creek railway. Paintings include sailing ships, praus, introduced buffalo and other game, revolvers and guns.

Main Location of Art Sites

Oenpelli-East Alligator River: The most important sites are at Inyalak Hill and Inagurdurwil, in the Arnhem Land Aboriginal Reserve. They are not endangered by development. However, natural causes are resulting in serious deterioration and they are unlikely to survive unless special measures are taken to preserve them.

Cooper and Tin Camp Creeks Region: There are many important sites in this remote region which is largely undisturbed. Because of its isolation Mt Borrodaile is outstanding both in range and quality of art. Sites in this northern sector, including Black Rock in the Wellington Range, may prove to be more important than those in the south such as in the region of Jim Jim Falls.

Obiri Rock: There is an excellent gallery of well-preserved paintings on a rock-face above a high ledge which has protected them from animals. In nearby rock shelters there is an extensive frieze depicting men in motion running across the wall. The attitudes and actions of the figures show a surprising variety, as do the weapons and other items that they are carrying or using.

Comparison of the several hundred sites examined in the Alligator Rivers Region has resulted in the conclusion that the Obiri paintings are some of the best examples in Arnhem Land and amongst the best in Australia.

The outstanding composition of the art, the clustering of many sites in a limited area, ready access, and natural protection afforded the paintings by extensive rock overhangs, make this area ideal for cultural tourist development.

192

Cannon Hill-Hawk Dreaming: This area is an extension of the group of sandstone residuals at Obiri. It is a region where there was continuous Aboriginal occupation until at least the 1920's. The rich natural environment has resulted in an equally rich heritage of Aboriginal art.

The densest concentration of sites is on Hawk Dreaming, an outlier on which twenty-two shelter sites are located. On top there is an extensive arrangement of stones. One shelter known as the 'Small Labyrinth', is at the northern end, and nearby is a cave with walls covered with large engravings. An interesting example of *Mimi* art is a picture of a small canoe with two figures poling it over a lagoon. One of the finest examples of art in the area is a freshwater crayfish in red ochre.

Particularly good examples of *Mimi* art occur on Hawk Dreaming, such as a battle scene in an excellent state of preservation and running figures with spears and spear-throwers. The paintings include also a row of brolgas with fish in their mouths, women with well-formed breasts, and grotesque spirit figures. One gallery has a naturalistic representation of a spider, an unusual subject.

Paintings of contact subjects are included in many galleries. Depicted amongst traditional art are paintings of steel axes, ships (one with portholes, sails and a cabin) rifles, pistols, a cowboy, Sydney Harbour bridge, a cat and an air force bomber.

Paintings in some of the galleries of the eastern outliers have been badly damaged by buffaloes; other galleries in the region are deteriorating through weathering, water damage, abrasive wind-blown sand and mould.

In places paintings appear high up on inaccessible cliff-faces. Many of the areas have been used as burial places. One frieze on the eastern outlier depicts men and women hunting and dancing and another a ceremony with a group of performers and a seated didjeridu player.

The nearby Birndu site has many galleries with paintings in a range of styles.

Mt Brockman-Nourlangie Rock massif: There are two main concentrations of art sites, Mt Brockman itself, which is a feature of sacred significance and Nourlangie Rock where there are numerous painted galleries.

The Mt Brockman sites are located in boulders at the base of the mount. The most important cave to Aborigines is known locally as 'Serpent Cave'. This has a large serpent painted in thick layers of red ochre on the back wall. The site also has beeswax figures and a large flat boulder with many distinctive cup-shaped grinding holes on its surface.

The largest Mt Brockman art complex has three galleries. *Mimi* figures, a large spirit figure, some polychrome figures and hand stencils characterize the site. There are fewer X-ray paintings, and contact paintings are almost absent.

As with its archaeological sites, the Mt Brockman series rates highly, and in some art types they are the best examples known.

The most impressive gallery in the Nourlangie Rock area depicts a group of stylized male and female spirit figures, surrounded by a number of polychrome paintings of legendary figures and some X-ray paintings. One of the figures is of a 'lightning man' who was responsible, in the Aboriginal world, for thunder, lightning, and associated storms. When he became angry he would strike the ground with his stone axes. He would shatter the trees, frighten the *Mimi* and sometimes kill people.

The Noranda Company has erected a wooden fence in front of the main gallery to keep people away from the paintings.

One shelter (Nangaloar), referred to as the 'ship cave', extends for seventy metres. There is a painting of a ship trailing a dinghy, others include totemic figures and X-ray fish. The site is visited regularly in the dry season by tourist buses but no steps have been taken to safeguard the site.

In one of the many small galleries in the area blue colouring, said to be Reckitts washing blue, has been used to paint traditional male and female figures.

Two small niches in an outcrop were used as burial chambers but ten skeletons formerly preserved there have all been stolen. A number of the paintings in the Nourlangie area have deteriorated badly but a small shelter called Djerlandjal Rock has a painting of a hunter and other figures, X-ray art and superimposed pictures, all of which are amongst the best-preserved paintings in the Alligator Rivers Region.

Nourlangie Rock is close to the main Arnhem Highway. With its picturesque features and waterholes, and concentration of Aboriginal art sites, it could be developed as a controlled tourist site with a resident ranger who could serve as a guide and protector of the art.

Deaf Adder Creek Valley: Art styles in this area range from early style red ochre paintings to *Mimi* art and X-ray, but contact paintings are less in evidence than in the northern areas.

There is a number of important sites. At Kolondjarluk Creek painted rock shelters extend for fifty metres, the site being important because it provides a representative selection of the main styles found in the Alligator Rivers Region. Most are well preserved being protected by overhanging cliffs. West of Deaf Adder Lagoon are numerous shelters, in one of them are interesting paintings of echidnas in X-ray style. The 'Lindner' archaeological site with carbon samples dated at 19 000 ± 280 BP is located in this area.

The most extensive and colourful single gallery is known as *Balawuru*. Paintings extend along the cliff for forty metres. Buffaloes caused damage until a protective fence was erected in 1972. The gallery includes about eighty human and 150 animal pictures and numerous others which have faded or been painted over. One painting is of a man using a rifle as if it were a spear. An interesting feature is the occurrence of cup-shaped depressions hammered into the surface of the walls, possibly associated with some past form of ritual.

There are interesting differences between *Mimi* paintings here and those at Oenpelli, but sometimes the two types are superimposed. The X-ray art includes paintings of human forms.

Mt Gilruth rises from the top of the plateau in this area. Over 200 metres of wall are covered with predominantly *Mimi* paintings and a few others in X-ray style. The art seems to be of great age and belongs to the earliest traditions in Arnhem Land.

The paintings in the Deaf Adder Creek Valley are some of the most significant in Australia, being associated with occupation for at least 19 000 years. Many of its features have been well protected and it is regarded as an area of great scientific value justifying intensive study and adequate protection.

The Main Escarpment: Sites were located between the East Alligator River crossing and the entrance to Deaf Adder Creek Valley. Most are minor and in a poor state of preservation. One major site is at Sawcut (Hickey) Creek where both paintings and rock engravings occur. It is also an Aboriginal sacred site.

Some important paintings, mainly featuring hunters and spirit figures, occur on outliers near the East Alligator River crossing.

The Plateau: Sites are known to exist on the plateau but this rugged and less accessible area has not been thoroughly surveyed as its isolation affords protection.

Jim Jim Creek: This is not a highly significant Aboriginal art area.

In summary rock art sites in the Alligator Rivers Region are dense, ranging from small galleries of a few paintings to large walls fifty or more metres long. The condition of the sites varies considerably. The more important clusters occur at Deaf Adder Creek Valley, the Mt Brockman-Nourlangie massif, Obiri Rock, Hawk Dreaming,

Cannon Hill and Oenpelli. Large sections of the escarpment lack significant areas of rock art, and the Jim Jim Creek region is less important than others to the north. Both Obiri Rock and Nourlangie Rock areas could be suitable for development as controlled cultural tourist sites.

Significance of rock art

Each site originally had an Aboriginal name and belonged to a particular Aboriginal group which had the rights of occupation and the responsibility for the maintenance of the paintings and for ceremonials associated with specific sites.

Paintings were made for different purposes and existing paintings are significant for various reasons.

Many paintings had a religious significance and were believed to be representations of legendary heroes of the Dreamtime, the spirit beings of creation. It was they who actually painted some of the images when they had completed their worldly tasks.

Retouching and repainting of these images is often a religious responsibility bestowed on certain groups or individuals. Once a tradition fades, or is lost, or those responsible disappear, a sacred site may lose some of its significance for the Aborigines. However, it may be an important study site warranting preservation. The centralization of Aborigines away from their tribal lands seems to be having this effect in the Alligator Rivers Region; for instance there are only a few people of the original *Kakadu* tribe of the area now known within the region.

Not all sites of significance to Aborigines have paintings associated with them. For instance of sixty four sacred sites recorded by Peter Carroll in the Nabarlek area, only six have paintings.

Mythology associated with paintings also has significance in more utilitatian ways. Some paintings bestow benefits such as the bringing of rain, or the increase of animals used for food. It is necessary to repaint such paintings to ensure this benefit.

Mountford records the legend of the Dreamtime activities of the water snake, a favourite food of the Aborigines. A design on the wall at Obiri Rock is said to have been painted by a mythological water snake (*Aniau-tjunn*). To increase the supply of water snakes Aborigines would lightly tap this painting so as to bring out the spirits of the water snakes which would then go to the lagoons and grow to large ones.

A feature of the Obiri cave is a painting of a spirit with his catch of fish. This is said to be *Nabarakbia* who stole the spirits of sick men or women and cooked and ate them. It was the duty of the medicine man to chase *Nabarakbia* away or the patients would die.

Some paintings have a day-to-day significance. For instance, they may represent a fish or animal a hunter wants to kill. By painting it on the wall he hopes to influence it so it will come where he can spear it; or it may be one that escaped and the painting is done as an inspiration to do better next time.

A man may paint the figure of a woman whose attention he would like, or if he has been successful to ensure that she remains faithful. Alternatively a woman's figure may be painted if she is unfaithful and she will fall sick and die as a result.

The significance of paintings differs considerably and there is need for studies in depth to isolate the different styles in this extremely large body of art. The Alligator Rivers Region galleries provide an excellent opportunity for study.

Where a succession of superimposed images has been built up there is a recorded history of customs and objects which can be expected to tell a great deal about the Aborigines' past, especially if studied in conjunction with excavated archaeological remains.

Damage and preservation of paintings

The need for permanence of the original pigments did not concern the Aboriginal artists, as regular retouching of paintings of significance was a traditional responsibility which required this to be done before rituals took place. This effectively preserved the images. Thus noticeable deterioration of rock art did not take place until Aborigines made contact with Europeans and their traditional cultures began to collapse.

Lack of retouching accompanying the abandonment of cave dwelling on a continuous basis now threatens many of the galleries. Evidence collected during the survey suggests that few Aborigines maintain traditional associations with the art of rock shelters.

Apart from this neglect and the natural processes of weathering, other natural factors are combining to hasten deterioration. These include water erosion and seepage, sometimes caused by rock cracking, tree growth in fissures, wasps nests on painted surfaces, termite clay trails, and feral animals rubbing against the paintings. Moulds grow in some of the more sheltered chambers. Bush fires fracture some surfaces and exfoliation changes others. Wind-borne sand abrades, and dust collects on paintings. The last has been intensified where present-day roads or tracks pass near painting sites.

Inaccessibility has minimized vandalism but experience elsewhere suggests that as numbers of visitors increase the inevitable writing or carving of names and other forms of damage could become serious unless adequate protective measures are adopted.

The rock art of the region, which is of a quality and quantity to make it of world importance, will not persist unless special efforts are made to protect it from both natural and man-made forms of deterioration.

Conclusion

Evidence for Aboriginal occupation of the region is represented by Aboriginal sites of significance, archaeological relics and rock art. The studies undertaken as part of the Alligator Rivers Region Environmental Fact Finding Study have indicated clearly the presence and the significance of many sites, and the necessity for investigations to be made through the appropriate channels when developments are proposed so that these features of Aboriginal culture may be adequately respected and perpetuated.

The archaeological studies confirmed the great significance of prehistoric sites in this region for the study of the long occupation by Aborigines and for their potential in providing data concerning the reconstruction of environmental conditions since the arrival of man. The studies so far have concentrated on the areas most likely to be near possible developments and they have adequately indicated the existence of sites which might need protection.

The survey of rock art, although by no means considered exhaustive, has recorded the existence of actual sites in even greater detail and furthermore has gone a long way to perpetuate the art in numerous photographic records of extremely high quality. The report establishes the importance of rock art in the context of world art and its significance in relation to archaeology and to the cultural traditions of the Aborigines.

Both studies have defined many factors in the environment, natural and man-made, which can lead to deterioration of these resources. The information provided should give a satisfactory basis for the planning of future attitudes to these important aspects of the Australian heritage.

References

Arndt, W. 1962 The interpretation of the Delemere lightning paintings and rock engravings. *Oceania,* 32(3) 163-177.

Attenborough, D. 1963 *Quest under Capricorn.* London. Lutterworth.

Berndt, R.M. 1970 *The sacred site. The western Arnhem Land example.* Canberra, Australian Institute of Aboriginal Studies.

Berndt, R.M. *and* C.H. Berndt 1951 *Sexual behaviour in western Arnhem Land.* New York, Viking Fund. (Viking Fund publications in anthropology, no. 16.)

Berndt, R.M. *and* C.H. Berndt 1954 *Arnhem Land: its history and its people.* Melbourne, Cheshire.

Berndt, R.M. *and* C.H. Berndt 1964 *The world of the first Australians.* Sydney, Ure Smith.

Berndt, R.M. *and* C.H. Berndt, *eds,* 1965 *Aboriginal man in Australia.* Sydney, Angus and Robertson.

Berndt, R.M. *and* C.H. Berndt 1970 *Man, land and myth in north Australia.* Sydney, Ure Smith.

Bowler, J.M. *et al.* 1970 Pleistocene human remains from Australia: a living site and human cremation from Lake Mungo, western New South Wales. *World Archaeology,* 2(1): 39-60.

Brandl, E.J. 1968 Aboriginal rock designs in beeswax and description of cave painting sites in western Arnhem Land. *Archaeology and Physical Anthropology in Oceania,* 3(1): 19-29.

Brandl, E.J. 1972 Aboriginal traditional sites in the Mudginbarry-Mount Brockman Area. Report to Northern Territory Administration Research Branch (Welfare Division).

Brandl, E.J. 1973 *Australian Aboriginal paintings in western and central Arnhem Land.* Canberra, Australian Institute of Aboriginal Studies.

Breuil, H. *and* L. Berger-Kirchner 1961 Franco-Cantabrian rock art. *In* H.G. Bandi *et al.* eds, *The art of the stone age.* Art of the World Series no. 5. London, Baden-Baden.

British Information Services 1972 Britain and international tourism, London. Her Majesty's Stationery Office.

Brown, G.B. 1905 *The care of ancient monuments.* Cambridge, Cambridge University Press.

Cadell, F.W. 1867 Exploration Northern Territory. Adelaide, Govt. Pr. (South Australian Parliamentary Paper no. 178).

Campbell, T.D. *et al.* 1966 Archaeological excavation in the south coast of South Australia. Typescript manuscript, (*In* A.I.A.S. manuscript collection).

Carroll, P.J. 1973 Investigation of twelve Aboriginal or 'sacred' sites at Nabarlek and preliminary survey of Aboriginal sites of significance in western Arnhem Land outside the Nabarlek area. Report to the Department of the Northern Territory.

Christian, C.S. 1973 A review report of the Alligator Rivers Region Environmental Fact Finding Study. Darwin.

Cole, E.K. 1972 *Oenpelli pioneer.* Melbourne, Church Missionary Historical Publications. (Great Australian missionaries, no. 4.)

Colliver, F.S. 1970 A survey of monuments and antiquities in Queensland. *In* McCarthy, F. D., *ed. Aboriginal antiquities in Australia:* 2-14.

Conigrave, C.P. 1936 *North Australia.* London, Cape.

Cooper, H.M. 1943 *Large stone implements from South Australia.* South Australian Museum. Records, &(4): 343-369.

Cooper, H.M. 1960 *The archaeology of Kangaroo Island, South Australia.* South Australian Museum. Records. 13(4): 483-503.

Crawford, I.M. 1968 *The art of the Wandjina.* Melbourne, Oxford University Press.

Dampier, William 1698 *A new voyage round the world.* London, James Knapton.

Dashwood, C.J. 1897 Government Resident report on the Northern Territory.

Davidson, D.S. 1936 *The spearthrower in Australia.* American Philosophical Society Proceedings, v. 74.

Davidson, D.S. 1936 *Aboriginal Australian and Tasmanian rock carvings and paintings.* American Philosophical Society. Memoirs, 5: 108-120.

Davidson, D.S. 1952 Notes on the pictographs and petroglyphs of Western Australia and a discussion of their affinities with appearances elsewhere on the continent. American Philosophical Society. Proceedings, v. 96.

De Telega, S. *and* W. Bryden 1958 A note on Tasmanian Aboriginal drawings. *Royal Society of Tasmania, Papers and Proceedings,* 92: 191.

Duncan, R. 1967 *The Northern Territory pastoral industry 1863-1910.* Melbourne, Melbourne University Press.

Dyer, A.J. 1960 The story of A.J. Dyer: experiences in Arnhem Land 1915 to 1934. Typescript manuscript (*In* A.I.A.S. manuscript collection).

Edwards, R. 1965 Rock engravings and Aboriginal occupation at Nackara Springs in the north-east of South Australia. *South Australian Museum Records.* 15(1): 9-27.

Edwards, R. 1968 Prehistoric Rock Engravings at Thomas Reservoir, Cleland Hills, western Central Australia. *South Australian Museum. Records,* 15(4): 647-670.

Edwards, R. 1971 Art and Aboriginal prehistory: *In* Mulvaney, D.J. *and* J. Golson, *eds, Aboriginal man and environment in Australia:* 356-367.

Edwards, R. 1972 Cultural tourism — the overseas example *In* National Seminar on Aboriginal antiquities in Australia. Report: 97-115. (now published as *The preservation of Australia's Aboriginal Heritage,* 1975, Canberra, Australian Institute of Aboriginal Studies.)

Edwards, R. *and* L. Manyard 1967 Prehistoric art in Koonalda Cave. *Royal Geographical Society of Australasia, South Australian Branch. Proceedings,* 68: 11-17.

Edwards, R. *and* P.J. Ucko 1973 Rock art in Australia. *Nature,* 246(5430): 274-277.

Elkin, A.P. 1938 *The Australian Aborigines: how to understand them.* Sydney, Angus and Robertson.

Elkin, A.P. 1964 Art and life. *In* Berndt, R.M., *ed. Australian Aboriginal art:* 11-19.

Elkin, A.P., Berndt, C.H. *and* R.M. Berndt, 1950 *Art in Arnhem Land.* Melbourne, Cheshire.

Ellis, R.W. 1972 South Australia: existing legislation and its implementation. *In* National Seminar on Aboriginal Antiquities in Australia. Report. (*See* Edwards, R. 1975 also.)

Evans, E.C. 1964 Patrol to establish road link between Oenpelli and Maningrida. *Australian Territories,* 4(2): 12-19.

Favenc, E. 1888 *The history of Australian exploration.* Sydney, Turner and Henderson.

Flinders, M. 1814 *A voyage to Terra Australis,* v. 1. London, Nicol.

Flood, J.M. 1970 A point assemblage from the Northern Territory. *Archaeology and Physical Anthropology in Oceania,* 1(1): 27-52.

Gould, R.A. 1968 Preliminary report on excavations at Puntutjarpa Rockshelter, near the Warburton Ranges, Western Australia. *Archaeology and Physical Anthropology in Oceania,* 3(3): 161-185.

Goyder, G.W. 1869 Copy of Surveyor-General's report on the survey of Northern Territory. Adelaide, Govt. Pr. (South Australian Parliamentary Paper no. 157).

Grant, C. 1967 *Rock art of the American Indian.* New York, Crowell.

Grey, G.E. 1841 *Journals of two expeditions of discovery in north-west and Western Australia during the years 1837, 38 and 39,* v. 1 London, Boone.

Hale, H.M. *and* N.B. Tindale 1930 Notes on some human remains in the lower Murray Valley, South Australia. *South Australian Museum, Records.* 4(2): 145-218.

Hall, F.J. *et al.* 1951 Aboriginal rock carvings: a locality near Pimba, South Australia. *South Australian Museum. Records,* 9(4): 375-380.

Harris, Kerr, Forster and Company 1969 Ayers Rock-Mt Olga National Park Development Plan. Hawaii.

Heeres, J.E. 1899 *The part borne by the Dutch in the discovery of Australia 1606-1765.* London, Luzac.

Hooper, A.D.L. 1969 Soils of the Adelaide-Alligator area. Melbourne, C.S.I.R.O. (Land Research Series no. 25).

Howard, F. 1866 Preceedings of survey schooner 'Beatrice'. Adelaide, Govt. Pr. (South Australian Parliamentary Paper no. 79).

Kamminga, J. *and* H. Allen 1973 Report of the archaeological survey *In* Alligator Rivers Environmental Fact-Finding Study.

King, P.P. 1827 *Narrative of a survey of the intertropical and western coasts of Australia.* London, J. Murray. 2v.

Lefevre, M. *and* G.S. Laporte 1969 The 'maladie verte' of Lascaux. *Studies in Speleology,* 2(1).

Leichhardt, L. 1846 Report of the expedition from Moreton Bay to Port Essington. *The Sydney Australian,* 26 March, 1846.

Leichhardt, L. 1847 *Journal of an overland expedition in Australia, from Moreton Bay to Port Essington.* London, T. and W. Boone.

Love, J.R.B. 1930 Rock paintings of the Worrora and their mythical interpretation. *Royal Society of Western Australia. Journal.* 16: 1-24.

Love, J.R.B. 1936 *Stone-age bushmen of today.* London. Blackie.

McBryde, I. 1968 Archaeological investigations in the Graman District. *Archaeology and Physical Anthropology in Oceania,* 3(2).

McCarthy, F.D. 1958 *Australian Aboriginal rock art*. Sydney, Australian Museum.

McCarthy, F.D. 1961 Rock engravings of Depuch Island, north west Australia *Australian Museum. Records,* 25(8): 145.

McCarthy, F.D. 1962 *Australian Aboriginal decorative art* 6 ed. Sydney, Aust. Museum.

McCarthy, F.D. 1962 The rock engravings of Port Hedland, north-western Australia. *Pap. Kroeber Anthrop. Society,* 26: 1-73.

McCarthy, F.D. 1964 The art of the rock faces. *In* Berndt, R.M. *ed. Australian Aboriginal art:* 33-43.

McCarthy, F.D., *ed.* 1970 *Aboriginal antiquities in Australia: their nature and preservation.* Canberra, Australian Institute of Aboriginal Studies.

McCarthy, F.D. and F.M. Setzler 1960 The archaeology of Arnhem Land. *American-Australian Scientific Expedition to Arnhem Land, Records.* 2: 215-295.

McConnel, U. 1953 Native arts and industries on the Archer, Kendall, and Holroyd rivers, Cape York Peninsula, North Queensland. *South Australian Museum. Records,* 11(1): 1-42.

Macintosh, N.W.G. 1951 Archaeology of Tandandjal Cave, south-west Arnhem Land. *Oceania,* 21: 178-213.

Macintosh, N.W.G. 1952 Paintings in Beswick Creek cave, Northern Territory. *Oceania,* 22: 256-274.

Macintosh, N.W.G. 1965 Dingo and horned anthropomorph in an Aboriginal rock shelter. *Oceania,* 36: 85-101.

McKinlay, J. 1866 Expedition of Northern Australia, Adelaide, Govt. Pr. (South Australian Parliamentary Paper no. 131).

Macknight, C.C. *ed.* 1969 *The farthest coast.* Melbourne, Melbourne University Press.

Masson, E.R. 1915 *An untamed territory.* London, Macmillan.

Mountford, C.P. 1954 *Australia: Aboriginal paintings — Arnhem Land.* New York, N.Y., Graphic Society (UNESCO world art series).

Mountford, C.P. 1955 The lightning man in Australian mythology. *Man,* 55:129-130.

Mountford, C.P. 1956 Art, myth and symbolism. *American Australian Scientific Expedition to Arnhem Land, Records,* v. 1.

Mountford, C.P. 1960 Simple rock engravings in Central Australia. *Man,* 60: 1-5.

Mountford, C.P. 1965 *Ayers Rock: its people, their beliefs and their art.* Sydney, Angus and Robertson.

Mountford, C.P. 1968 *Winbaraku and the myth of Jarapiri.* Adelaide, Rigby.

Mulvaney, D.J. and E.B. Joyce 1965 Archaeological and geomorphical investigations on Mt Moffatt Station, Queensland, Australia. *Proc. prehist. Soc.,* 31: 147-212.

Mulvaney, D.J. 1969 *Prehistory of Australia.* London, Thames and Hudson.

Mulvaney, D.J. and J. Golson, *eds,* 1971 *Aboriginal man and environment in Australia.* Canberra, Australian National University Press.

National Seminar on Aboriginal Antiquities in Australia. *Canberra, 23-24 May 1972.* Report. (*See* Edwards, R. 1975).

National Trust 1969 Annual report, London, Waterlow and Sons.

Ovington, J.D. *et al,* 1973 A study of the impact of tourism at Ayers Rock-Mt Olga National Park. Australian Publishing Service.

Parsons, J.L. 1885 Quarterly report on Northern Territory. Adelaide, Govt. Pr. (South Australian Parliamentary Paper no. 53).

Petrie, C.C. 1904 *Tom Petrie's reminiscences of early Queensland.* Brisbane, Watson.

Polach, H.A. *et al.* 1968 A.N.U. radiocarbon date list II. *Radiocarbon,* 10(2): 179-199.

Rudner, J. and I. Rudner 1970 *The hunter and his art.* Cape Town, Struik.

Simpson. C., 1951 *Adam in ochre.* Sydney, Angus and Robertson.

Spencer, W.B. 1914 *Native tribes of the Northern Territory.* London, Macmillan.

Spencer, W.B. 1928 *Wanderings in wild Australia,* v. 2. London, Macmillan.

Stanner, W.E.H. 1960 Aboriginal rock paintings. *Etruscan,* 9(4): 18-23.

Stockdale, H. 1891 South Australian Archives no. 790, 791.

Stockdale, J. 1789 *The voyage of Governor Phillip to Botany Bay.* London, Stockdale.

Stokes, J.L. 1846 *Discoveries in Australia with an account of the coast and rivers explored and surveyed dyring the voyage of the H.M.S. Beagle in the years 1837-43.* London, Boone.

Strehlow, T.G.H., 1964 The art of circle, line and square. *In* Berndt, R.M. *ed. Australian Aboriginal Art:* 44-59.

Thomson, D.F. 1949 *Economic structure and the ceremonial exchange cycle in Arnhem Land.* Melbourne, Macmillan.

Tindale, N.B. 1928 Native rock shelters at Oenpelli, Van Diemen Gulf, North Australia. *South Australian Naturalist,* 9(2): 35-36.

Tindale, N.B. 1959 Totemic beliefs in the western desert of Australia. Part 1. Women who became the Pleiades. *South Australian Museum, Records.* 13(3): 306-332.

Trezise, P.J. 1969 *Quinkan country.* Sydney, Reed.

Trezise, P.J. and R.V.S. Wright 1966 The durability of rock-paintings on Dunk Island, northern Queensland. *Mankind,* 6(7): 320-324.

Turner, D.H. 1973 Rock art of Bickerton Island in comparative perspective. *Oceania.* 43: 286-325.

Walston, S. 1972 Rock art: deterioration and conservation *In* National Seminar on Aboriginal Antiquities in Australia. Report. (*See* Edwards, R. 1975).

Warburton, C.W. 1934 *Buffaloes.* Sydney, Angus and Robertson.

Washington, G. 1972 Australia's tourist potential *In* National Seminar on Aboriginal Antiquities in Australia. Report. (*See* Edwards, R. 1975.)

White, C. 1967 Early stone axes in Arnhem Land. *Antiquity* 41(162): 149-152.

White, C. 1967 The prehistory of the Kakadu people. *Mankind,* 6(9): 426-431.

White, C. 1967 Plateau and plain: prehistoric investigations in Arnhem Land, Northern Territory. Ph.D. thesis, Australian National University, Canberra (unpublished).

White, C. *and* N. Peterson 1969 Ethnographic interpretation of the prehistory of western Arnhem Land. *Southwestern Journal of Anthropology,* 25(1): 45-67.

White, C. 1971 Man and environment in northwest Arnhem Land *In* Mulvaney, D.J. *and* J. Golson, *eds, Aboriginal man and environment in Australia:* 141-157.

Wilson, T.B. 1835 *Narrative of a voyage around the world.* London, Sherwood, Gilbert and Piper.

Wright, B.J. 1968 *Rock art of the Pilbara region, north-west Australia.* Canberra, Australian Institute of Aboriginal Studies.

Wright, B.J. 1970 Observations of damage and comments on the preservation of Aboriginal art sites in the Pilbara district of north-western Australia. *In* McCarthy, F.D., *ed. Aboriginal antiquities in Australia:* 121-125.

Wright, R.V.S. 1971 Prehistory in Cape York Peninsula. *In* Mulvaney, D.J. *and* J. Golson, *eds, Aboriginal man and environment in Australia:* 133-140.